# Stem Cell Research and Cloning

POINT ||||||
\||||| COUNTERPOINT

**Affirmative Action**
**Amateur Athletics**
**American Military Policy**
**Animal Rights**
**Capital Punishment**
**DNA Evidence**
**Election Reform**
**The FCC and Regulating Indecency**
**Fetal Rights**
**Freedom of Speech**
**Gay Rights**
**Gun Control**
**Immigrants' Rights After 9/11**
**Immigration Policy**
**Legalizing Marijuana**
**Mandatory Military Service**
**Media Bias**
**Mental Health Reform**
**Miranda Rights**
**Open Government**
**Physician-Assisted Suicide**
**Policing the Internet**
**Protecting Ideas**
**Religion in Public Schools**
**The Right to Privacy**
**Rights of Students**
**Search and Seizure**
**Smoking Bans**
**Stem Cell Research and Cloning**
**Tort Reform**
**Trial of Juveniles as Adults**
**The War on Terror**
**Welfare Reform**

# Stem Cell Research and Cloning

Alan Marzilli

SERIES CONSULTING EDITOR
Alan Marzilli, M.A., J.D.

CHELSEA HOUSE
PUBLISHERS

An imprint of Infobase Publishing

**Stem Cell Research and Cloning**

Chelsea House
An imprint of Infobase Publishing
132 West 31st Street
New York NY 10001

ISBN-10: 0-7910-9230-5
ISBN-13: 978-0-7910-9230-9

**Library of Congress Cataloging-in-Publication Data**
Marzilli, Alan.
  Stem cell research and cloning / Alan Marzilli.
    p. cm. — (Point/counterpoint)
  Includes bibliographical references and index.
  ISBN 0-7910-9230-5 (hardcover)
  1. Embryonic stem cells—Juvenile literature. 2. Embryonic stem cells—Research—Juvenile literature. 3. Embryonic stem cells—Research—Moral and ethical aspects—Juvenile literature. 4. Cloning—Juvenile literature. 5. Cloning—Moral and ethical aspects—Juvenile literature.  I. Title. II. Series.
  QH588.S83M37 2006
  174.2'8—dc22          2006017148

Chelsea House books are available at special discounts when purchased in bulk quantities for businesses, associations, institutions, or sales promotions. Please call our Special Sales Department in New York at (212) 967-8800 or (800) 322-8755.

You can find Chelsea House on the World Wide Web at
http://www.chelseahouse.com

Series design by Keith Trego
Cover design by Takeshi Takahashi

Printed in the United States of America

Bang FOF 10 9 8 7 6 5 4 3 2

This book is printed on acid-free paper.

All links and Web addresses were checked and verified to be correct at the time of publication. Because of the dynamic nature of the Web, some addresses and links may have changed since publication and may no longer be valid.

# CONTENTS

Foreword    6

INTRODUCTION

Miracle Cures or Moral Transgressions?    10

POINT

Supporters Exaggerate the Benefits of
Embryonic Stem Cell Research    18

COUNTERPOINT

Embryonic Stem Cell Research
Holds Great Promise    33

POINT

Embryonic Stem Cell Research Is Immoral    48

COUNTERPOINT

Embryonic Stem Cell Research Is Compatible
with Contemporary Moral Standards    69

POINT

Cloning for Any Purpose Is Immoral    88

COUNTERPOINT

Using SCNT to Create Embryos for Stem Cell
Research Is Morally Acceptable    104

CONCLUSION

The Future of Stem Cell Research    118

Notes    126

Resources    132

Elements of the Argument    135

Appendix: Beginning Legal Research    136

Index    140

# Foreword
**Alan Marzilli, M.A., J.D.**
**Washington, D.C.**

The debates presented in POINT/COUNTERPOINT are among the most interesting and controversial in contemporary American society, but studying them is more than an academic activity. They affect every citizen; they are the issues that today's leaders debate and tomorrow's will decide. The reader may one day play a central role in resolving them.

Why study both sides of the debate? It's possible that the reader will not yet have formed any opinion at all on the subject of this volume—but this is unlikely. It is more likely that the reader will already hold an opinion, probably a strong one, and very probably one formed without full exposure to the arguments of the other side. It is rare to hear an argument presented in a balanced way, and it is easy to form an opinion on too little information; these books will help to fill in the informational gaps that can never be avoided. More important, though, is the practical function of the series: Skillful argumentation requires a thorough knowledge of *both* sides—though there are seldom only two, and only by knowing what an opponent is likely to assert can one form an articulate response.

Perhaps more important is that listening to the other side sometimes helps one to see an opponent's arguments in a more human way. For example, Sister Helen Prejean, one of the nation's most visible opponents of capital punishment, has been deeply affected by her interactions with the families of murder victims. Seeing the families' grief and pain, she understands much better why people support the death penalty, and she is able to carry out her advocacy with a greater sensitivity to the needs and beliefs of those who do not agree with her. Her relativism, in turn, lends credibility to her work. Dismissing the other side of the argument as totally without merit can be too easy—it is far more useful to understand the nature of the controversy and the reasons *why* the issue defies resolution.

The most controversial issues of all are often those that center on a constitutional right. The Bill of Rights—the first ten amendments to the U.S. Constitution—spells out some of the most fundamental rights that distinguish the governmental system of the United States from those that allow fewer (or other) freedoms. But the sparsely worded document is open to interpretation, and clauses of only a few words are often at the heart of national debates. The Bill of Rights was meant to protect individual liberties; but the needs of some individuals clash with those of society as a whole, and when this happens someone has to decide where to draw the line. Thus the Constitution becomes a battleground between the rights of individuals to do as they please and the responsibility of the government to protect its citizens. The First Amendment's guarantee of "freedom of speech," for example, leads to a number of difficult questions. Some forms of expression, such as burning an American flag, lead to public outrage—but nevertheless are said to be protected by the First Amendment. Other types of expression that most people find objectionable, such as sexually explicit material involving children, are not protected because they are considered harmful. The question is not only where to draw the line, but how to do this without infringing on the personal liberties on which the United States was built.

The Bill of Rights raises many other questions about individual rights and the societal "good." Is a prayer before a high school football game an "establishment of religion" prohibited by the First Amendment? Does the Second Amendment's promise of "the right to bear arms" include concealed handguns? Is stopping and frisking someone standing on a corner known to be frequented by drug dealers a form of "unreasonable search and seizure" in violation of the Fourth Amendment? Although the nine-member U.S. Supreme Court has the ultimate authority in interpreting the Constitution, its answers do not always satisfy the public. When a group of nine people—sometimes by a five-to-four vote—makes a decision that affects the lives of hundreds of millions, public outcry can be expected. And the composition of the Court does change over time, so even a landmark decision is not guaranteed to stand forever. The limits of constitutional protection are always in flux.

These issues make headlines, divide courts, and decide elections. They are the questions most worthy of national debate, and this series aims to cover them as thoroughly as possible. Each volume sets out some of the key arguments surrounding a particular issue, even some views that most people consider extreme or radical—but presents a balanced perspective on the issue. Excerpts from the relevant laws and judicial opinions and references to central concepts, source material, and advocacy groups help the reader to explore the issues even further and to read "the letter of the law" just as the legislatures and the courts have established it.

It may seem that some debates—such as those over capital punishment and abortion, debates with a strong moral component—will never be resolved. But American history offers numerous examples of controversies that once seemed insurmountable but now are effectively settled, even if only on the surface. Abolitionists met with widespread resistance to their efforts to end slavery, and the controversy over that issue threatened to cleave the nation in two; but today public debate over the merits of slavery would be unthinkable, though racial inequalities still plague the nation. Similarly unthinkable at one time was suffrage for women and minorities, but this is now a matter of course. Distributing information about contraception once was a crime. Societies change, and attitudes change, and new questions of social justice are raised constantly while the old ones fade into irrelevancy.

Whatever the root of the controversy, the books in POINT/ COUNTERPOINT seek to explain to the reader the origins of the debate, the current state of the law, and the arguments on both sides. The goal of the series is to inform the reader about the issues facing not only American politicians, but all of the nation's citizens, and to encourage the reader to become more actively involved in resolving these debates, as a voter, a concerned citizen, a journalist, an activist, or an elected official. Democracy is based on education, and every voice counts—so every opinion must be an informed one.

On July 19, 2006, just before this book went to press, President George W. Bush vetoed the Stem Cell Research Enhancement Act, which would have expanded federal funding for a controversial type of research. Embryonic stem cell research involves growing human cells in a laboratory for medical purposes. It is controversial for two main reasons. First, the process begins with the destruction of human embryos, which many people equate with murder. Supporters of the research, however, believe that the potential for cures derived from this research justifies the destruction of embryos that are created in a laboratory and in the first days of their existence.

The second major criticism of embryonic stem cell research is the charge that it is unlikely to produce cures anytime soon, and that alternatives, such as growing "adult stem cells," which are taken harmlessly from a living person, are superior. Many scientists, however, think that embryonic stem cells, though a newer and unproven technology, have an enormous potential for developing cures for a variety of medical conditions.

This volume also examines a closely related technology often called "therapeutic cloning." In this procedure, scientists create an embryo that is an exact genetic copy of a living animal—it has not yet been done successfully in humans—and use cells taken from that embryo for stem cell research. Cloning is even more controversial because it sidesteps natural means of reproduction and raises fears of mass production of "lesser" humans to be used for the convenience of others.

President Bush's veto left intact the funding policy that is discussed in this volume, and the debates over embryonic stem cell research and cloning continue at the state and federal levels.

# Miracle Cures or Moral Transgressions?

Before the mid-1990s, actor Christopher Reeve was best known for playing Superman in a series of movies, and actor Michael J. Fox was famous for the "Back to the Future" movies and a string of successful television roles. However, twists of fate brought the two actors into the public spotlight for less fortunate reasons.

On May 27, 1995, Reeve, who had always enjoyed adventure and had become a competitive horseback rider, fell from his horse. A severe injury to his spinal column left him paralyzed from the neck down, and he became one of the estimated 250,000–400,000 Americans with spinal cord injuries. Although scientists have not discovered a cure for the paralysis caused by spinal cord injuries, extensive physical rehabilitation helps many people with such injuries regain some mobility. In addition to the devastation that spinal cord injuries cause to the

Christopher Reeve poses for photographers with his wife Dana, above, as he arrives at the thirteenth annual Christopher Reeve Paralysis Foundation gala event in New York on November 24, 2003. Reeve was paralyzed in a horseback-riding accident; before his death in 2004, he raised a great deal of money for spinal cord research, including stem cell studies.

people harmed and their families, the financial costs to care for people with spinal cord injuries are enormous, with spending for care far outpacing spending on research for cures. With a determination to overcome his disability and to help others do so, the actor founded the Christopher Reeve Foundation to raise money for spinal cord research and to raise public awareness of the issue. Reeve died on October 10, 2004, but his foundation continues its efforts, with Reeve as a symbol of the foundation's urgent mission.

Like Reeve, Michael J. Fox became determined to use his fame to help campaign for a cure. Also like Reeve, he started a foundation bearing his name to fund research. In 1998, Fox announced to the public that he suffers from Parkinson's disease, with which he was diagnosed in 1991. Parkinson's disease is a progressive neurological disorder. It affects the brain and nervous system, and symptoms worsen over time. One of the more common symptoms is tremors, or uncontrolled shaking, although other symptoms can include stiffness, weakness, and difficulty walking or talking. As with spinal cord injury, scientists have found ways to treat Parkinson's disease, but have not found a cure. Doctors can treat Parkinson's disease with various drugs, which often have unpleasant side effects, and some experimental surgical procedures have also been used to relieve symptoms. Although these treatments show some success in reducing the symptoms, they do not cure Parkinson's disease.

Reeve and Fox became two of the most visible spokespeople for a new field of research that some say offers scientists the greatest hope yet for finding a cure for paralysis, Parkinson's disease, and a host of other conditions such as diabetes, cancer, Lou Gehrig's Disease (ALS), and other debilitating and life-threatening diseases. With the development of embryonic stem cell technology in 1998, a buzz began to sound in the scientific community, which the popular media and politicians soon began to pick up. Soon, news reports and campaign speeches were full of references to this latest "miracle cure."

## What are stem cells?

The human body contains millions of cells of countless shapes, sizes, and functions. Liver cells, skin cells, hair cells, blood cells—the list goes on and on. However, each person was at one point a single cell: a fertilized egg, which forms when a sperm cell fuses with an egg cell. This one cell begins to divide and differentiate, meaning that as the cells continually split in twos, the resulting cells are not like the cells from which they came. In this way, all of the somatic cells (body cells) form from the original cells of the embryo, which at one point contained one, then two, then four, then eight cells, and so on.

Scientists realized that these original cells of the embryo in the earliest stage of its existence must be incredibly versatile, as they develop into so many different types of cells in the body. They coined the term pluripotent ("having many powers") to describe this capacity. They use the term "stem cell" to refer to a type of cell that not only has this function—to produce various types of additional cells—but also has the ability to replicate itself. Because stem cells are able to self-replicate, scientists can grow stem cell lines—large supplies of identical cells that can be studied.

## What types of stem cells exist?

Embryonic stem cells are the most widely discussed type of stem cell. They have the ability to replicate themselves indefinitely in the laboratory and the ability to generate any type of cell in the human body. The mystery lies in how scientists can coax stem cells into forming various types of cells. Embryonic stem cells are taken from an early-stage embryo, four to five days old, a process which results in the destruction of the embryo.

A common source of embryos for this process is fertility clinics. Couples who are not able to conceive a child often resort to in vitro fertilization (IVF), which involves collecting the woman's eggs and the man's sperm and fertilizing the eggs with the sperm in the laboratory. The resulting embryos, which can continue to divide for about 14 days in laboratory conditions, are implanted into the woman's uterus. Because the procedure is expensive and not always successful, couples typically create more embryos than they need and freeze the extras for future tries. (At this early stage of their existence, embryos can survive the freezing and unfreezing process.) Many couples, whether or not they have been successful in having children, end up with extra embryos, which they donate for research purposes. Scientists can use these donated embryos as a source of embryonic stem cells.

Adult stem cells are sometimes called post-natal ("after birth") stem cells, because they are found throughout the bodies of children and adults. These cells have as their natural function the creation of other cells that the body needs to replenish. For example, stem cells in the bone marrow replenish the body's supply of blood cells. Other adult stem cells are found in the nervous system and various organs. Stem cells may also be found in fetuses and the umbilical cord that connects mother to baby, which is cut at birth. Adult stem cells reproduce in a living person, and recent research suggests that adult stem cells also have the ability to replicate indefinitely in the laboratory. Although adult stem cells generally produce a single type, or a limited number of types, of cell in the human body, research indicates that, like embryonic stem cells, it is possible to manipulate adult stem cells into developing various types of cells.

Another possible source for stem cells is "cloned" embryos. Scientists have made exact genetic copies of animals such as sheep by taking the genetic material from an adult cell and injecting it into a hollowed-out egg cell, using a process called somatic cell nuclear transfer (SCNT). Unlike the normal fertilization process, which unites the genetic material of two parents, the resulting embryo has the same genes as the parent. Some speculate that SCNT could be a powerful tool for embryonic stem cell therapies, as scientists could replace a person's damaged or missing cells with new cells that are genetically identical. In other words, cells from a person with a spinal cord injury could be cloned, and stem cells removed from the resulting embryo could be used to grow new spinal tissue that would have the person's own genes.

## What are the current and projected uses of stem cells?

The medical profession has used adult stem cells in treatment for many years. Bone marrow transplantation is an effective technique to treat various forms of cancer. Additionally, autologous bone marrow transplantation (in which a person's own bone marrow is removed and then later transplanted) is used after cancer chemotherapy or radiation treatment that might destroy a person's bone marrow.

However, with conditions such as Parkinson's disease, spinal cord injuries, diabetes, heart disease, and many others, the problem is that cells are damaged or missing and are not replenished by the adult stem cells of the human body. For example, an injured spinal cord does not heal itself by regrowing tissue. Therefore, scientists have begun experimenting with ways of manipulating adult stem cells to replace missing cells.

Many, though not all, researchers believe that embryonic stem cells have greater potential to form the types of cells that could be useful in treating diseases and injuries. In nature, embryonic stem cells are much more versatile in the types of cells that they form than are adult stem cells. Also, isolating adult stem cells can be difficult.

## Why are embryonic stem cells controversial?

Despite the perceived advantages of embryonic stem cells over adult stem cells, research with embryonic stem cells is highly controversial. Creating a stem cell line—though the cells replicate themselves indefinitely—must begin with the step of destroying an embryo during the early days of its existence. For some people, this act poses no moral problem. The collection of stem cells takes place at a time well before the embryo takes on a human form and well before the stage at which legal abortions take place. However, many people believe that human life begins at the moment the egg is fertilized, and because the destruction of the embryo to harvest the stem cells takes place after fertilization, many people regard embryonic stem cell research as the moral equivalent of murder.

### Why is cloning, or SCNT, controversial?

Harvesting embryonic stem cells from cloned embryos raises the same moral objection to destroying embryos as do other forms of embryonic stem cell research. However, the process of cloning itself is also controversial. Many people believe that by experimenting with cloning, scientists are "playing God." Opponents also worry that cloning could create a class of subordinate humans denied the respect they deserve, and they fear the potential for such practices as "organ farming"—making a clone simply so that its organs can be taken for transplantation.

### Is embryonic stem cell research legal?

In the United States, federal law does not prohibit embryonic stem cell research. In August 2001, President George W. Bush approved limited federal funding for embryonic stem cell

## THE LETTER OF THE LAW

## South Dakota Prohibits Embryo Research, Including Creating Embryonic Stem Lines

No person may knowingly conduct nontherapeutic research that destroys a human embryo. A violation of this section is a Class 1 misdemeanor....

The term, nontherapeutic research, means research that is not intended to help preserve the life and health of the particular embryo subjected to risk....

The term, human embryo, means a living organism of the species Homo sapiens at the earliest stages of development (including the single-celled stage) that is not located in a woman's body.

Source: South Dakota statutes, secs. 34-14-16, 34-14-19, 34-14-20.
  © State of South Dakota

research. Funds are available only for research using embryonic stem cell lines that were in existence at the time of the announcement—about two dozen. Researchers have clamored for additional funding, saying that the usefulness of these earlier stem cell lines is limited. Legislators in both the Senate and House of Representatives have proposed various bills that would either limit embryonic stem cell research or provide additional federal funding.

At the state level, several states, such as South Dakota, have criminalized embryonic stem cell research, and others limit state funding. At the other extreme, some states have approved state funding for research ineligible for federal funding, with California voters approving a multibillion-dollar stem cell initiative.

## Is cloning legal?

To date, a human has not been cloned, but legislators have been active in preparing for such a possibility. No federal law prohibits cloning, although members of both houses have proposed legislation that would ban cloning altogether or that would allow it for the purposes of medical research and treatment but not for the purpose of giving birth to a cloned child. At the state level, a number of states have banned cloning for any purpose. In other states, efforts to ban cloning have failed.

## Summary

Embryonic stem cell research and developing cloning technology have generated both widespread enthusiasm and deep moral concerns. This volume examines several topics of current debate. First, will embryonic stem cells have true potential, or are they the latest in a long line of overly hyped "miracle cures"? Second, do moral objections to embryonic stem cell research justify bans or strict limits on the technology? Third, should cloning be allowed for research purposes or prohibited for any reason?

# Supporters Exaggerate the Benefits of Embryonic Stem Cell Research

Sixteen-year-old Laura Dominguez was on the way home from school with her brother when a chance oil spill on the highway changed her life forever. The siblings were involved in a severe car accident that fractured one of Laura's vertebrae (bones in the neck), damaging her spinal cord and leaving her paralyzed from the neck down. Unwilling to accept that she would never walk again, Laura and her family immediately began seeking anything that could help. They learned about a surgical procedure that was not being performed in the United States but was being pursued by a surgical team in Portugal—a procedure that involved adult stem cells.

During the surgery, doctors removed stem-cell-containing tissue from Laura's olfactory sinus, the tissue responsible for the sense of smell. These cells are a type of adult stem cell that are found throughout the body and not taken from embryos.

The doctors injected the cells directly into the damaged area of Laura's spinal column. After a period of recovery, an MRI (magnetic resonance image, similar to an x-ray) revealed that about 70 percent of the damage to her spinal cord had healed—a remarkable result, because the spinal cord does not regenerate itself naturally.

With intensive physical therapy and unwavering dedication to walking again, Laura began to regain function. Eventually, she was able to walk 1,400 feet with the assistance of braces. She told a Congressional committee:

> I have regained more feeling and movement. Some of the movements that I am able to make are functions that are controlled by the very tip of my spinal cord. Although the intensive physical training that I had enhanced my ability to regain strength and movement, prior to surgery I did not have the type of function and feeling that I have now.[1]

Stories like Laura's are remarkable. Proponents say embryonic stem cell research will lead to many stories like hers. During the 2004 presidential campaign, John Edwards and John Kerry made an issue out of embryonic stem cell research, arguing that the technique could one day help people like paralyzed actor Christopher Reeve walk again.

However, it is important to remember that Laura was not helped by the embryonic stem cells promoted by the Kerry-Edwards campaign, but by adult stem cells, which can be safely taken from adults or children. So far, the "miracles" promised of embryonic stem cells have not materialized. Critics point to the lack of a track record for embryonic stem cell research, coupled with promising results in adult stem cell research, to argue that the limited amount of funding that society has to devote to medical research should go to adult stem cell research. Arguing against expanded funding of embryonic stem cell research, critics say that President Bush's policy, which allows federal funding for research

on stem cell lines developed prior to August 2001, provides suf-
ficient funding for scientists to discover whether embryonic stem
cells will ever live up to the hype.

## Embryonic stem cells have not proven effective.

Although proponents of research bill embryonic stem cells as
a "sure thing" for curing paralysis, Parkinson's disease, diabetes, and other conditions, opponents argue that support for
embryonic stem cell research is pure hype. A fact sheet released
by Michigan Right to Life contains a typical statement: "Embryonic stem cell research has yet to cure a single patient of a single
disease. . . . Proponents have created a fairy tale, promising that
cures are at the fingertips of scientists when this isn't the case."[2]
The Do No Harm Coalition, a group of scientists opposed to
embryonic stem cell research, cloning, and other techniques
that its members consider unethical, keeps a running score-
card on its Web site, tallying the number of conditions treated
with adult stem cells versus those treated with embryonic stem
cells. As of February 2006, the tally was 65 to 0 in favor of adult
stem cells.[3]

Even with a lack of research documenting the effectiveness of
embryonic stem cell research, California voters adopted a measure in 2004 that devoted billions of dollars to embryonic stem
cell research. Critics blasted the measure as an unwise move for
a state that had had ongoing budget problems. Before the vote,
Scott Gottleib of the conservative American Enterprise Institute criticized Californians for considering a multibillion-dollar
initiative that would pump government money into biotechnology companies that had not been found promising by private
investors. Noting that "the persistent enthusiasm for stem cells
has outpaced their scientific legitimacy," he argued, "It is just not
apparent that messing around with embryonic stem cells and all
their associated ethical baggage is all that necessary"[4] —in other
words, given the lack of demonstrated success with embryonic
stem cells and the widespread moral objections to it, spending a

tremendous amount of money on embryonic stem cell research is not a smart decision.

Discussing federal funding, Father Kevin Wildes of Georgetown University testified to the National Bioethics Advisory Commission (NBAC):

> One must also ask about the questions of justice in devoting resources, especially national resources, to such research when there are so many other basic medical and health needs that are unmet.[5]

Critics also point out that, in addition to a lack of demonstrated success, the use of embryonic stem cells poses a risk to patients. Testifying to Congress, Jean Peduzzi-Nelson warned that early experiments with embryonic stem cells have shown that the risk of tumors is very real:

> In an animal model of Parkinson's disease, rats injected with embryonic stem cells showed a slight benefit in about 50% of the rats, but one-fifth (20%) of the rats died of brain tumors caused by the embryonic stem cells. This was confirmed in another similar study conducted by a different group of researchers who also found tumor formation in about 20% of the rats.

Another potential problem with cells generated by embryonic stem cells is the possibility of rejection by the patient's immune system. Scientists at the Children's Hospital of Pittsburgh working with adult stem cells noted:

> The use of embryonic stem cells could be complicated by issues of rejection, with the recipient's immune system rejecting the foreign embryonic stem cells. With [adult] stem cells taken from the recipient and then reintroduced in an autologous manner, rejection would not be an issue.[6]

While many people agree that embryonic stem cells have the potential to provide cures, a significant number of people argue that problems such as tumors and immune rejection, together with the vast amount of work that would have to be done to understand how to turn embryonic stem cells into specific needed cells, make embryonic stem cell research an unworthy pursuit that should be abandoned in favor of adult stem cell treatment.

## Adult stem cells hold greater promise for cures.

For years, researchers have known that the adult body contains stem cells, which, like embryonic stem cells, have the ability to form various types of other cells. The most widely studied adult stem cells have been hematopoeic stem cells (HSCs), which are found in the bone marrow and naturally function to form blood cells. Stem cells have also been isolated from the brain, spinal cord, pulp of the teeth, muscles, skin, digestive tract, and other organs.

For quite some time, doctors have performed bone-marrow transplants, which essentially replace HSCs in people whose own supply has been depleted or damaged due to certain diseases or cancer treatments. These treatments rely on stem cells—specifically, HSCs—doing what they naturally do in the human body, which in this case is producing blood cells.

More recently, scientists have had success in developing treatments that capitalize on the ability of stem cells to generate new cells. Scientists have discovered that some of the stem cells naturally occurring in the human body do not produce new cells as a course of nature. However, by intervening, scientists are able to make these stem cells produce new cells. Neurosurgeon and medical researcher Michel Levesque described how his laboratories have developed a method for using adult stem cells to replace cells in the central nervous system:

Since 1996, our laboratories have been involved with the isolation and characterization of human adult-derived neural stem cells, obtained from patients undergoing neurosurgical procedures. In the adult brain, these cells cannot on their own trigger repair responses. However, if placed in experimental laboratory conditions stimulating certain genes, these neural stem cells can be "awakened" and begin to divide and replicate events of normal development.

These newly created neural stem cells can grow for several months in laboratory conditions reaching several millions in number, a process called cell expansion. Their ability to self-replicate and form all types of cells found in the central nervous system can be verified in vitro under controlled conditions. They can be placed in storage or maintained in sterile incubators until ready for use.[7]

His team developed the technique as a treatment for Parkinson's disease, which is caused by the failure of brain cells to produce the hormone dopamine. Parkinson's disease is currently incurable; it is characterized by progressively worsening symptoms. Although the technique has not been tested on a widespread scale, Levesque has transplanted cells derived from a Parkinson's patient's own stem cells into that patient, who showed a remarkable recovery from Parkinson's disease.

While saying that further studies are needed, Levesque believes that his technique of autologous transplantation—meaning that cells derived from the patient's own stem cells are transplanted into that patient—will prove superior to using embryonic stem cells to manufacture dopamine-producing cells for Parkinson's patients. Embryonic stem cells, which have the capability of forming many types of cells, he explained, may be difficult to turn into dopamine-producing cells. He also warned that the versatility of the embryonic stem cells—touted as their greatest asset—could also be a liability, argu-

**Actor Michael J. Fox, center, addresses members of the media during a press conference at which he urged members of the U.S. Congress to pass legislation supporting funding for stem cell research. Fox suffers from Parkinson's disease, which many believe might be curable with innovations in the use of stem cells.**

ing that their "possible transdifferentiation into other types of tissue" had the potential to cause "tumors, immune reactions in the host brain and questionable functional benefits."[8] In other words, the ability of embryonic stem cells to form any type of cell in the human body poses a great danger if scientists cannot be certain how to stop this shape-shifting ability once the new cells are introduced into the body.

One of the highest-profile advocates of adult stem cell research is David Prentice. Now a senior fellow at the Family Research Council, a conservative organization, he prepared a background paper on adult stem cells for the President's Council on Bioethics while he was a professor at Indiana State University. In the background paper, which is included in the council's report on stem cells, Prentice outlined a number of examples of how adult stem cells can form various types of cells. Citing numerous studies, largely conducted on animal models, he suggested that human bone-marrow stem cells can form cells of the liver, skin, digestive tract, brain, retina of the eye, muscles, kidneys, pancreas, and heart. He also suggested that neuronal (from the nervous system) stem cells could be used for conditions involving the brain or nervous system. His background paper concluded:

> In summary, our current knowledge regarding adult stem cells has expanded greatly over what was known just a few short years ago. Results from both animal studies and early human clinical trials indicate that they have significant capabilities for growth, repair, and regeneration of damaged cells and tissues in the body, akin to a built-in repair kit or maintenance crew that only needs activation and stimulation to accomplish repair of damage. The potential of adult stem cells to impact medicine in this respect is enormous.[9]

People associated with conservative causes, like Prentice, are not the only supporters of adult stem cell research; however, fellow conservatives have pushed strongly for expansion of adult stem cell research, which they say has the dual advantage of proven effectiveness and the absence of a need to destroy embryos. Organizations such as Concerned Women for America, the Family Research Council, and the Do No Harm Coalition have released fact sheets to their members touting the applications of adult stem cells. In addition to treatments for Parkinson's disease and spinal cord injuries, some of the cures touted as established or under study include transplantations of insulin-producing cells from cadavers to treat diabetes, adult stem cells to treat multiple sclerosis (MS), bone marrow cells to treat heart disease, bone marrow cells to treat liver failure, and umbilical cord blood cells to treat acute myeloid leukemia (AML).

## Proponents of embryonic stem cell research are motivated by money and exploit the suffering.

Proponents of embryonic stem cell research frequently argue that opponents, especially those who support adult stem cell therapies, are motivated more by religious belief than by scientific facts or concern for suffering individuals. However, opponents point out that the supporters of embryonic stem cell research have their own ulterior motive: money. Of course, many people suffering from serious diseases or disabling conditions also support embryonic stem cell research. Critics do not accuse the ill of having an ulterior financial motive. Instead, they argue that the ill have been made a pawn of money-hungry researchers and corporate interests.

In a Congressional hearing about the benefits of adult stem cell research, Jean Peduzzi-Nelson, a medical professor, argued that the embryonic stem cell industry had clouded the issue, making anyone who opposes embryonic stem cell research out to be a religious zealot. She testified:

> Some people naively think that the stem cell controversy is just related to the abortion issue, political party alignment, religious beliefs, or scientific freedom. However, none of these are the driving force in the effort to promote Federal funding of human embryonic stem cells or human cloning.[10]

While acknowledging that religion might be a motivating factor in opposition to embryonic stem cell research, her point is that supporters of embryonic stem cell research have capitalized on the religious nature of the opposition to make it seem as though opponents of embryonic stem cell research have an ulterior motive, while their own motives are pure. Peduzzi-Nelson argued that this is not the case: "The most profitable, not the best, treatment for people is being promoted. The main reason for the current emphasis on human embryonic stem cells and cloning is money."[11]

Peduzzi-Nelson explained why money might motivate people to promote funding of embryonic—as opposed to adult—stem cell research. She said that the distinction is that embryonic stem cells can be used to create genetic commodities that could be sold—U.S. patent law allows researchers to patent the stem cells they develop, meaning that they have the exclusive right to sell and profit from particular stem cell therapies. She testified:

> It is a superior business plan to have a mass-produced product such as embryonic/fetal/cloned stem cells that can be sold nationwide and have patentable intellectual property. Cloned stem cells derived from embryos with genetic defects represent the possibility of millions in patentable stem cell lines.[12]

By contrast, because adult stem cell therapies rely on using an individual patient's own cells, any discoveries that are made in the area have limited commercial potential because the stem cells are useful only to the individual patient. Further, because the procedure is not patentable, the innovator of an adult stem cell therapy does not have the right to charge others for using the innovation. The result, Peduzzi-Nelson said, is:

> Adult stem cell therapies are much better for people with diseases or injuries but generate an inferior business plan. In the case of adult stem cells where, in most cases, a person's own cells can be used, one can only develop a procedure that is generally not patentable according to new patent laws.[13]

In a policy brief about adult stem cell research, the conservative group Concerned Women for America noted a similar concern. The brief accuses supporters of embryonic stem cell research of having conflicts of interest. It singles out several well-known researchers affiliated with universities but also having ties to for-profit biotech companies that "would thrive with government funding"[14] of embryonic stem cell research. The brief commented, "The media have quoted these 'experts' hundreds of times regarding their support of [embryonic stem cell research], but rarely mention their financial stake in the debate."[15]

Writing in *Commonweal* magazine, Daniel Callahan of the Hastings Center points out that scientists have in the past asked for vast sums of money for projects, such as mapping human genes, that have yielded few results, remarking, "Nor will scientists usually mention this, living as they do off grant money, but they will do well even if nothing comes of the research."[16] He, however, stopped short of accusing scientists of corruption, admitting, "Serious scientists would not want the money if they did not see some good coming of it, either advances in knowledge or useful clinical applications."[17]

The commercial motives of those who support embryonic stem cell research have been raised not only by supporters of adult stem cell research but also by fiscal conservatives—people who believe that the government should spend less money and lower taxes. In the conservative *American Spectator* magazine, senior editor Tom Bethell writes that the hype in favor of embryonic stem cell research is reminiscent of the National Institute of Health's Human Genome Project, which was a massive, heavily funded project to map human genes. Once the Human Genome Project was funded, Bethell laments, "little more was heard of the disease-curing potential of the genome sequence," and he predicts, "A similar scenario will probably unfold with embryonic stem cells."[18]

Michael Tanner of the Cato Institute, a libertarian think-tank calling for a very limited federal government, agrees that the debate over embryonic stem cell research "is really a fight about money" and "a perfect example of how science becomes politicized when government money is involved."[19] His solution is for the government to wash its hands of the stem cell debate. Noting that most important scientific and medical breakthroughs are made by private companies, he writes, "Those people calling for increased funding could take out their checkbooks and support it. Those who oppose embryonic stem cell research would not be forced to pay for it."[20]

Of course, much of the support for embryonic stem cell research comes from people with serious medical conditions. People with diabetes want a life without insulin injections or the risk of complications. People with spinal cord injuries want to walk again. People with ALS (Lou Gehrig's disease) want to end the deadly course of their disease. These people do not have economic motives, but critics of embryonic stem cell research accuse researchers of making the suffering unwitting pawns in their quest for stem cell funding.

Some have accused lobbying groups of misinforming their members of the benefits of embryonic stem cell research and understating the benefits of adult stem cells. *National Review* senior editor Rammesh Ponnuru wrote a column telling the story of an Indiana man who had accompanied his two diabetic granddaughters to Washington, D.C. They met with Indiana Congressman Mark Souder, an opponent of embryonic stem cell research, in a meeting arranged by the Juvenile Diabetes Research Foundation (JDRF), armed with information and literature provided by JDRF. The two girls told their stories about living with diabetes and asked the representative to support embryonic stem cell research. Ponnuru noted that such appeals to members of Congress are common and effective because of the "discomfort that most congressmen feel when people in distress cry in their offices."[21] Souder stood his ground, Ponnuru reports, and even convinced the family to support adult stem cell research and oppose embryonic stem cell research. The lesson, he suggests, is that "all the citizen lobbyists who have gone to the Capitol" might not "have the full story on this issue. . . ."[22]

Critics have also accused politicians of exploiting the suffering in the stem cell debate. During the 2004 presidential campaign, Democratic challenger John Kerry made an issue of President Bush's limitations on funding for embryonic stem cell research. Charles Krauthammer is one of the many who accused the Kerry campaign of distorting the issue of stem

## President Bush Announces Federal Stem Cell Funding Policy

*On August 9, 2001, President George W. Bush announced the first-ever federal funding of embryonic stem cell research. The policy, however, limited funding to research with stem cell lines that were already in existence at the time of the announcement so that federal funding would not encourage the destruction of additional embryos.*

As a result of private research, more than 60 genetically diverse stem cell lines already exist. They were created from embryos that have already been destroyed, and they have the ability to regenerate themselves indefinitely, creating ongoing opportunities for research. I have concluded that we should allow federal funds to be used for research on these existing stem cell lines, where the life-and-death decision has already been made.

Leading scientists tell me research on these 60 lines has great promise that could lead to breakthrough therapies and cures. This allows us to explore the promise and potential of stem cell research without crossing a fundamental moral line, by providing taxpayer funding that would sanction or encourage further destruction of human embryos that have at least the potential for life.

I also believe that great scientific progress can be made through aggressive federal funding of research on umbilical cord placenta, adult and animal stem cells which do not involve the same moral dilemma. This year, your government will spend $250 million on this important research.

I will also name a president's council to monitor stem cell research, to recommend appropriate guidelines and regulations, and to consider all of the medical and ethical ramifications of biomedical innovation. This council will consist of leading scientists, doctors, ethicists, lawyers, theologians and others and will be chaired by Dr. Leon Kass, a leading biomedical ethicist from the University of Chicago.

This council will keep us apprised of new developments and give our nation a forum to continue to discuss and evaluate these important issues. As we go forward, I hope we will always be guided by both intellect and heart, by both our capabilities and our conscience.

cell research. Krauthammer is a member of the President's Council on Bioethics, and a conservative columnist. He is also a physician who has been paralyzed since medical school. In a column for *townhall.com,* Krauthammer accused Kerry and his running mate, John Edwards, of exploiting Christopher Reeve and of "posthumous exploitation" of Ronald Reagan's then-recent death from Alzheimer's disease. He wrote: "Politicians have long promised a chicken in every pot. . . . But to exploit the desperate hopes of desperate people with the promise of Christ-like cures is beyond the pale."[23]

### President Bush's policy offers adequate funding.

Opponents of embryonic stem cell research had a mixed reaction to President Bush's stem cell funding policy. Under the policy, announced on August 9, 2001, federal funding is available for research on stem cell lines created up until the date of the announcement, but not for stem cell lines created after that date. The rationale was that the policy would not create additional incentives to destroy embryos to create stem cell lines but would take advantage of the stem cell lines that had already been created. Many have criticized the policy, saying that no funding should go to embryonic stem cell research, even if no additional embryos have to be destroyed.

Others, however, have supported the policy as providing an adequate research base for embryonic stem cell research. During the 2004 presidential campaign, Leon Kass of the President's Council on Bioethics defended the policy from attacks by Kerry and Edwards. In a *Washington Post* editorial, Kass noted that the Bush administration had increased funding for embryonic stem cell research from nothing in 2001 to $24.8 million in 2003 and that ample supplies of embryonic stem cells were available to researchers: "Nearly 500 shipments of cells have already been made to researchers; 3,500 more sit ready for delivery upon request. There is no shortage of embryonic stem cells."[24]

Former Secretary of Health and Human Services Tommy Thompson also took to the editorial pages to defend the administration's funding policy. Writing in *USA Today*, Secretary Thompson noted that NIH had devoted significant resources to developing embryonic stem cell research and that private industry has also invested heavily in embryonic stem cell research. He advocated a wait-and-see approach before expanding funding, arguing that before the federal government could change the policy, "we must first exhaust the potential of the stem-cell lines made available within the policy, as well as the ability of the private sector to go beyond the policy."[25]

## Summary

The media and politicians have fueled the hype surrounding embryonic stem cell research, though embryonic stem cells have yet to cure a single person. Many believe that the government should support adult stem cell research to the exclusion of embryonic stem cell research, pointing out that adult stem cells already have proven applications. Critics question the motives of embryonic stem cell proponents, saying that they are mostly interested in making money from "inventions" derived from human life. The federal government currently provides limited funding for embryonic stem cell research, and some say this funding is enough to let scientists prove whether embryonic stem cells will turn out to be effective, or just hype.

# Embryonic Stem Cell Research Holds Great Promise

**R**esearchers at the University of California–Irvine (UCI) have been working diligently to help find a cure for the paralysis caused by spinal cord injury. In a person with a spinal cord injury, cells called oligodendrocytes die at the site of the injury. The UCI researchers believed that the key to repairing the injury was to inject the site of the injury with a type of cell called an oligodendrocyte progenitor cell (OPC) because it "gives birth" to oligodendrocytes. Experimenting with rats, the scientists took OPCs derived from human embryonic stem cells into the spinal cords of rats with spinal cord injuries. The results were striking: The treated rats were able to move their legs and bear weight. In effect, the embryonic stem cells were turned into "repair cells" that replaced the dead cells in the rat's spinal cords.

Proponents of embryonic stem cell research are still waiting for the day when they can introduce to the public someone who

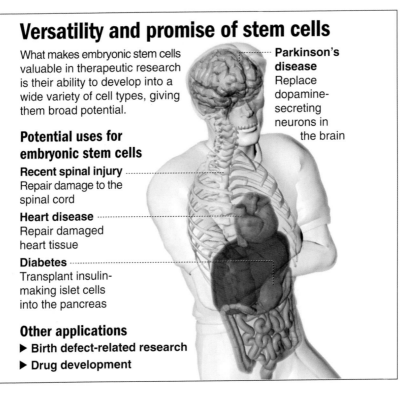

# Versatility and promise of stem cells

What makes embryonic stem cells valuable in therapeutic research is their ability to develop into a wide variety of cell types, giving them broad potential.

## Potential uses for embryonic stem cells

**Recent spinal injury**
Repair damage to the spinal cord

**Heart disease**
Repair damaged heart tissue

**Diabetes**
Transplant insulin-making islet cells into the pancreas

## Other applications
▶ **Birth defect-related research**
▶ **Drug development**

**Parkinson's disease**
Replace dopamine-secreting neurons in the brain

**Embryonic stem cells are unique in that they can grow into any type of cell in the human body. The graphic above illustrates the potential uses for stem cells in repairing damaged tissues of all types.**

has been cured using embryonic stem cells. While pointing to a rat that has regained its ability to walk does not have the same effect as curing a person, proponents say that scientists are making remarkable progress. Embryonic stem cell technology dates back only to 1998, and medically approved cures can take years from discovery through testing in animals, then humans, until approved for general use.

With time and, more importantly, with funding, proponents say, embryonic stem cell research holds enormous potential. Supporters point to the unique properties of embryonic stem cells to grow into any type of cell in the human body. All of the complex elements in our bodies are descended from these fundamental cells. The capacity of embryonic stem cells to form any type of cell, along with the relative ease of isolating embryonic stem cells, leads proponents to believe that one day embryonic stem cells will prove to be more versatile than the adult stem cells that today are being used for a number of therapies. Proponents find themselves fighting attacks from religious conservatives and those who accuse them of greed, but researchers maintain that they have the public good in mind. Ever since President Bush announced that funding would be available only for a limited number of older cell lines, researchers have been pushing for expanded funding for newer and better cell lines. With this funding, they say, cures never thought possible will be within their grasp.

## Embryonic stem cell research has enormous potential that requires financial support.

Many people in the scientific community firmly believe that embryonic stem cell research holds the best promise to cure a number of diseases and conditions, and they express their enthusiasm when they discuss the need for research. Although critics say that claims in support of embryonic stem cell research are inflated, most researchers tend to be cautious in the claims that they make. Some of the more lavish claims, such as that cures are right around the corner, appear to be more fabrications of politicians, the media, and advocacy groups than of the researchers who support the study of embryonic stem cells. Writing in the *Washington Post*, Johns Hopkins University researchers Ruth Faden and John Gearhart admit that supporters of embryonic stem cell research "sometimes seem to suggest that but for the [Bush] administration's policy, stem cell cures for dread diseases would already be in hand."[26] However, they urged readers not to let the inflated claims detract from the real issue: cures remain years away and limiting funding for embryonic stem cell research simply pushes the timeline back further.

Supporters of embryonic stem cells are extremely frustrated with opponents who argue that human embryonic stem cells have not been proven to cure any diseases. "Of course not," medical professors Gerald Fischbach and Ruth Fischbach write in the *Journal of Clinical Investigation*:

> Research is hampered by current regulations, and it is difficult to succeed with one hand tied behind one's back. As in all great scientific advances, it takes time and a great deal of money to translate fundamental discoveries into clinically useful treatments.[27]

# THE LETTER OF THE LAW

## California's Ambitious Stem Cell Initiative

**Article XXXV is added to the California Constitution to read:**

**SECTION 1**
There is hereby established the California Institute for Regenerative Medicine ("Institute").

**SECTION 2**
The Institute shall have the following purposes:

(a) To make grants and loans for stem cell research, for research facilities and for other vital research opportunities to realize therapies, protocols, and/or medical procedures that will result in, as speedily as possible, the cure for, and/or substantial mitigation of, major diseases, injuries and orphan diseases.

(b) To support all stages of the process of developing cures, from laboratory research through successful clinical trials.

(c) To establish the appropriate regulatory standards and oversight bodies for research and facilities development.

**SECTION 3**
No funds authorized for, or made available to, the Institute shall be used for research involving human reproductive cloning.

Despite the limitations, researchers have made some progress in the basic science of embryonic stem cells, a foundation that must be laid before the medical research can continue. Gearhart told Congress about some of the basic research that could one day lead to medical applications:

> Let me tell you what takes place now. We are able, for example,
> to grow large numbers of human heart muscle cells. We can

**SECTION 4**

Funds authorized for, or made available to, the Institute shall be continuously appropriated without regard to fiscal year, be available and used only for the purposes provided herein, and shall not be subject to appropriation or transfer by the Legislature or the Governor for any other purpose.

**SECTION 5**

There is hereby established a right to conduct stem cell research which includes research involving adult stem cells, cord blood stem cells, pluripotent stem cells and/or progenitor cells. Pluripotent stem cells are cells that are capable of self-renewal, and have broad potential to differentiate into multiple adult cell types. Pluripotent stem cells may be derived from somatic cell nuclear transfer or from surplus products of in vitro fertilization treatments when such products are donated under appropriate informed consent procedures. Progenitor cells are multipotent or precursor cells that are partially differentiated but retain the ability to divide and give rise to differentiated cells.

**SECTION 6**

Notwithstanding any other provision of this Constitution or any law, the Institute, which is established in state government, may utilize state issued tax-exempt and taxable bonds to fund its operations, medical and scientific research, including therapy development through clinical trials, and facilities....

Bonds in the total amount of three billion dollars ($3,000,000,000) . . . may be issued and sold to provide a fund to be used for carrying out the purposes expressed in this article.

Source: California Proposition 71 (2004).

do this now through embryonic stem cell technology. We are now in the process of grafting these cells into various animal models, whether it is congestive heart failure, heart attack, to see if these cells will function following transplantation. The same is true of dopaminergic neurons for Parkinson's disease or motor neurons. . . ."[28]

Although some people control their optimism more than others, proponents of embryonic stem cell research have suggested numerous uses for embryonic stem cells can be attained within the near future—although that future might be a decade down the road.

Researchers hope to cure some conditions by injecting cells derived from embryonic stem cells directly into patients. One example of a condition for which such a solution is proposed is spinal cord injuries. Scientists have conducted experiments with animals in which human embryonic stem cells have been injected into paralyzed laboratory animals, helping them regain movement.

Another example is a hoped-for treatment for type-1 diabetes, often called "juvenile diabetes" because it affects children and adolescents. In type-1 diabetes, the body stops producing insulin, which the body needs to process sugar and other carbohydrates. As a result, patients must—multiple times per day for the rest of their lives—carefully test their blood sugar and take insulin injections. Patients also face a number of potential complications, including blindness, kidney failure, and amputation of limbs. In a healthy person, insulin is produced by specialized cells called beta cells, which are thought to be destroyed by the body's immune system in people with type-1 diabetes. Scientists hope to coax embryonic stem cells into forming these insulin-producing beta cells, which could be injected into people with diabetes. Early results are under evaluation.

Scientists are also working to discover treatments for heart disease. Researchers hope to repair heart tissue damaged by heart attack or infection by injecting heart cells derived from embryonic stem cells. Researchers have developed heart cells from embryonic stem cells and injected them into laboratory animals.

Another way in which scientists suggest that human embryonic stem cells could be useful is to grow cells that mimic human diseases. The cells can be injected into animals to create animal models of the disease. Scientists can then test how experimental drugs interact with these cells in animal models before testing the drugs in humans.

## Adult stem cells do not hold the same promise as embryonic stem cells.

A favorite tactic of opponents of embryonic stem cell research is to push for the advancement of research with adult stem cells as an alternative. In cultivating stem cells from adult tissue, or from umbilical cord blood, no embryos are destroyed, and thus the research is morally acceptable to people holding a pro-life viewpoint. However, supporters of embryonic stem cell research reject the contention that the availability of adult and cord-blood cells in any way diminishes the need for research with embryonic stem cells.

First, supporters argue that embryonic stem cells are more versatile than adult stem cells, with the ability to generate more types of cells and tissue. Second, they argue that the success that adult stem cell research has yielded for some types of conditions does not apply to other conditions. Finally, they argue that research with adult cells should be done in addition to, rather than instead of, research with embryonic stem cells.

The primary argument against limiting research to adult stem cells is that many researchers believe that embryonic stem cells are more versatile than adult stem cells. These researchers say that embryonic stem cells have the ability to from any cell in the human body, while adult stem cells can only make a limited number of types of cells.

In a 2001 report on stem cells, the National Institutes of Health (NIH) noted that adult stem cells have been found in a variety of tissue. The most widely used in research and medicine have been HSCs, the stem cells derived from bone marrow. Other stem cells have been isolated in the blood, the brain, the pulp (the innermost part) of the teeth, the skin, the spinal cord, and organs such as the liver and pancreas. However, the key issue in the debate over their usefulness, the report noted, is plasticity, or the ability of stem cells from one source to make adult cells of a different type. An example of plasticity would be if HSCs from bone marrow were able to generate nerve cells as opposed to simply making blood cells. The NIH report concluded, "There is limited evidence that a single adult stem cell or genetically identical line of adult stem cells demonstrates plasticity"; however, "Rarely have experiments that claim plasticity demonstrated that the adult stem cells have generated mature, fully functional cells or that the cells have restored lost function in vivo."[29] In other words, there was limited evidence that adult stem cells could be used to create types of cells other than those the stem cells routinely created in the body.

Testifying before Congress several years later, Weissman noted that the plasticity of even the widely studied HSCs remained questionable:

> When the first reports of HSC transdifferentiation to regenerating heart cells, or brain cells, or liver cells, or skeletal muscle cells were reported I was excited that the HSC we had isolated might have much broader clinical uses than we had initially envisioned. So we embarked on experiments to repeat the original findings, hoping to make them better understood and easier and more efficient by improving the processes involved. But we found that we could not confirm blood-forming stem cells giving rise to brain, or heart, or liver, or skeletal muscle in a robust fashion.[30]

His experiments led him to conclude, "Adult tissue stem cells . . . can lead to robust regeneration, but only of the tissue from which they came."[31]

The lack of plasticity—that is, the inability to create many kinds of cells—is not the only problem identified with generating cells from adult stem cells. Some other technical problems with adult stem cells, according to Fischbach and Fischbach, make "adult stem cells less attractive than embryonic stem cells."[32] First, isolating adult stem cells can be difficult. Second, it is difficult to make adult stem cells continue to replicate themselves in the laboratory. Finally, as adult cells, they "have been exposed to a lifetime of environmental toxins and have also accumulated a lifetime of genetic mutations."[33]

Another major argument against limiting research to adult stem cells is that different diseases need different therapies and that success with adult stem cells in treating some diseases will not translate into success in other areas. One particular condition for which supporters say embryonic stem cells provide greater hope for a cure is type-1 diabetes. The Juvenile Diabetes Research Foundation (JDRF), while continuing to fund research involving adult stem cells, has poured research funding into embryonic stem cell research.

Referring to earlier testimony about using adult stem cells to treat Parkinson's disease, Robert Goldstein of JDRF told a Congressional committee that there was no way to predict whether that success would translate into successful treatment of other conditions. He testified:

> Adult stem cells may one day prove to be the answer to alleviating the pain and suffering caused by certain diseases—I certainly hope that is the case. We have heard some remarkable stories from some of the witnesses today. But we have no idea of knowing which diseases those may be, and unfortunately we are not certain of the widespread application of these treatments. We do know that to date, adult stem cells have not been shown to hold as much promise for juvenile diabetes as embryonic stem cells.[34]

In his testimony, Goldstein reviewed some of the research that had been done with both adult and embryonic stem cells. He noted that some research indicated that adult stem cells taken from the pancreas and bone marrow had the potential to develop into insulin-producing beta cells. He also discussed research that suggested that embryonic stem cells had the potential to develop into beta cells. He noted that opponents of embryonic stem cell research had latched on to the results with adult stem cells, even though they were not conclusive, but urged Congress not to cut off embryonic stem cells as an avenue of exploration: "JDRF takes the position that research using both embryonic and adult stem cells, perhaps even in side-by-side comparisons, will get us to our goal fastest."[35]

Most supporters of embryonic stem cell research, in fact, argue that adult stem cell research and embryonic stem cell research both deserve support. Indeed, John Wagner, whose research is limited to adult stem cells and stem cells derived from umbilical cord blood, testified at the same hearing that he believed it was necessary for others to be investigating embryonic stem cells:

> It must be unequivocally clear that our work in cord blood and adult stem cells does not eliminate the need for work in [embryonic stem] cells. Yes, it is true that stem cells and cord blood and adult tissues can differentiate into perhaps the lining cells of the gut or the liver or neural tissue, but they do not exhibit all the capacities of [embryonic stem] cells. For example, we have yet to see stem cells from cord blood or adult tissues differentiate into heart muscle that spontaneously beats in the petri dish. That has been shown repetitively by people working on [embryonic stem] cells.[36]

Some have accused opponents' support of adult stem cells as a "red herring," or false argument that detracts attention from the real issue. Although both embryonic stem cells and adult stem cells are indeed types of stem cells, conducting research on embryonic stem cells does not prohibit research on adult stem cells, so the issue is not truly an "either-or" debate. Medical professor Steven Teitelbaum testified to Congress:

Opponents of embryonic stem cell research often articulate their position as a contest between adult and embryonic stem cells. Mr. Chairman, this is not a contest between various types of stem cells. It is a contest between us as a society and disease. We should be moving forward on all fronts, adult, embryonic, and umbilical cord stem cells, to win the battle. The tool is not important. What counts is curing our neighbors.[37]

## Supporters of embryonic stem cell research have the public good in mind.

In the debate over embryonic stem cell research, both supporters and opponents have questioned the motives of those on the other side of the debate. Supporters have defended themselves against accusations that they are interested only in money, saying that their motivations are to help people. In turn, research supporters accuse opponents of supporting adult stem cells based on religious motivation rather than sound science.

While critics say that people are interested in developing embryonic stem cell lines because they can be patented and sold to other researchers, supporters say that limiting federal funding only makes the problem worse. In effect, because the developers of the stem cell lines eligible for federal funding have "cornered the market," it allows them to charge higher fees for use of the cell lines. Curt Civin, a cancer researcher at Johns Hopkins University, told Congress that he had been frustrated by having to go through negotiations and paying higher-than-expected fees. He expressed the need for greater access to stem cell lines, which could be developed using federal funding:

> Many scientists have similar stories to tell. . . .We all believe that stem cell research has tremendous potential to deliver treatments and cures. I believe that the pressure should be on us as stem cell researchers to turn that potential into treatments for our patients. With research, we can make stem cells that are self-renewing, that are less likely to be rejected by the recipient's immune system, and which regenerate a variety of

engineered tissues and organs that might even perform better than the originals. As a scientist, I want to get started. I want to bring these benefits to my patients and others. I do not want to limp along. I want other scientists to enter this field. I want to be spurred on by their advances.[38]

On the other hand, supporters of embryonic stem cell research question the motives of those who would fund only adult stem cell research to the exclusion of embryonic stem cell research. Fischbach and Fischbach single out Richard Doerflinger, of the U.S. Conference of Catholic Bishops, who has been one of the staunchest proponents of adult-cells-only policies. Noting that Doerflinger has highlighted research findings to support his arguments that adult stem cells could accomplish what embryonic stem cells could, Fischbach and Fischbach write: "The passion behind Doerflinger's statement is laudable, but it must be recognized that it is based on religious conviction, not on scientific induction or verified data."[39]

## President Bush's policy hinders important research.

The federal policy announced by President Bush in August 2001 has made few people happy. While pro-life critics maintain that no embryo research should be funded, research supporters say that the limited number of cell lines eligible for federal funding severely limits useful research because of a number of practical problems. As Civin's testimony indicates, researchers had to pay relatively large licensing fees for using the initial stem cell lines. Other problems identified by critics of the policy include difficulties obtaining the cells, problems growing the stem cells, possible contamination of the cell lines, and the superiority of cell lines developed later. As a result of all of the problems with the cell lines eligible for funding under the Bush policy, Senator Hillary Clinton said, only about 20 stem cell lines are available for federally funded research, instead of the 78 lines promised at the time Bush announced his policy. Clinton criticized the policy, saying that this number is insufficient:

It's clear that the administration's policy is far more restrictive than it appeared when first announced. And the limited number of cells available for federal funding means that we are not fully achieving the promise of these cells for research into many chronic, debilitating and fatal conditions.[40]

One reason that the number of cell lines has been less than originally expected is that not all of the researchers who developed the cell lines have been eager to share them with other researchers. In addition to the fees charged, Civin testified that bureaucratic hurdles had gotten in the way. He told the Congressional panel that he had had difficulty negotiating with the owners of one cell line how much royalties the owners would receive on future research and that after months of negotiating with a company in India over the right to use seven federally approved stem cell lines, the Indian government prohibited the company from exporting the stem cells.

For those who have obtained the cells, he said, the experience has been disappointing. Civin recounted the experience of a colleague who was able to obtain some of the federally approved cells:

These cells grow exceedingly slowly, one-tenth the rate of the cells we usually work with. So it has taken my colleague more than four additional months of incremental steps until he has been able to grow enough ES cells to perform even preliminary experiments.[41]

An additional problem that Gearhart, the other Johns Hopkins researcher, noted  is potential contamination of the cell lines, which were developed prior to August 2001, using older technology that relies on mouse cells to grow the human embryonic stem cells. He told Congress:

Since 2001, we have learned that all the NIH-approved stem cell lines were isolated in contact with mouse "feeder" cells.

The possibility of contamination in these lines compromises their quality [and] makes their therapeutic use in humans uncertain. . . .[42]

While noting that researchers in the United States and a number of other countries had developed new cell lines that did not use the mouse feeder cells, he lamented that federally funded researchers cannot use these newer lines.

An additional advantage to stem cell lines developed later—lines that are not eligible for federally funded research—is that some of them have been specifically developed to study certain diseases. Larry Goldstein of the University of California, San Diego, noted that stem cell lines had been developed that contain the genetic mutation that causes Huntington's disease, a progressive and fatal disorder of the nervous system. He suggested:

The ability to develop brain cells from those cells that have those genetic changes will let us understand what fails early in the disorder and could be an incredibly important tool in solving the problems of that disease.[43]

The federal stem cell funding policy has resulted in great inefficiency, critics charge. Researchers must choose between funded research on the potentially inadequate cell lines and unfunded research on the newer cell lines. Trying to conduct both types of research results in an administrative burden, Goldstein said:

If we are using the approved lines for NIH funding in our laboratories, they must be handled in a very, very different way logistically than lines that we use from Harvard or from Singapore in that it must be clear that everything that touches those cells, including the technicians that are using it, has a straight line and only a straight line to the federal funding source, that there is no crossover into other areas of where that federal money is going. That logistically is a nightmare.

Most of us have to build separate laboratories to make sure that those walls are there. This is a major, major limitation.[44]

While researchers struggle along, critics say, the clock is ticking for those who suffer from debilitating or fatal conditions. Expressing frustration with critics who point to the lack of demonstrated cures using embryonic stem cells, John Wagner testified to Congress:

> Is this all hype? Where are the first trials with ES cells? Certainly the lack of funding and restricted access to suitable stem cell lines has been a major barrier in our research efforts. We need to address those barriers where possible. . . . If you desire rapid translation of [embryonic stem] cells into real clinical therapies, let us not restrict it.[45]

## Summary

To date, nobody has been cured by embryonic stem cell research, but supporters say that, as with any new technique, time is needed to perfect it before it can be used to cure people. In the meantime, they argue, their progress is being slowed by the Bush administration's policy of funding research only on stem cell lines developed before 2001, which—if available at all—have numerous problems. While not denying the usefulness of adult stem cells, proponents of embryonic stem cell research say both areas should be pursued, and that by making embryonic stem cells widely available, suffering people will benefit more than the biotechnology companies.

# Embryonic Stem Cell Research Is Immoral

**W**aiting for an important package to arrive can be stressful. Finding out that it has been mistakenly delivered to a warehouse can be frustrating. But as Donielle Brinkman told the Wisconsin legislature, when that package contains your children, the experience can be heart-wrenching. Although people for years have spoken of a stork bringing their babies, Brinkman is one of the few people who can say that her baby was brought by a Fed-Ex truck. Brinkman and her husband Jim, after unsuccessful attempts to conceive their own child, applied to the Snowflakes adoption program. The program, which has received support from President George W. Bush, matches people who want to adopt a baby with frozen embryos created by couples who had planned to use them to get pregnant but no longer want them for that purpose. Rather than letting them perish, the couples allow them to be adopted through the Snowflakes program. The

**48**

Brinkmans' son Tanner was born on May 22, 2001, thanks to the Snowflakes program.

Many people believe that stories like Tanner's are too few and far between and would like to see more people able to adopt the estimated 400,000 embryos suspended in time in a deep-freeze, originally created by infertile couples but no longer needed or wanted by those couples to try to carry to term as their own children. This supply—some would say "population"—of frozen embryos has become a major point of contention in the debate over embryonic stem cells. Proponents of embryonic stem cell research believe that these "unwanted" embryos should be used for research to help others. Opponents, while not suggesting that adopting all 400,000 is possible, believe that the embryos are human lives and should not be destroyed, no matter what type of discoveries might follow from that.

The primary source of moral objections to embryonic stem cell research has been the pro-life movement. Consisting largely of fundamentalist and conservative Protestants and Roman Catholics, the pro-life movement pushes for laws that protect human life at all stages, from the beginning of life to natural death. The main goal of the pro-life movement continues to be restricting, and eventually outlawing, abortion, as the pro-life movement considers abortion to be tantamount to murder. Pro-life advocates typically believe that life begins at fertilization, when sperm and egg join, resulting in a new organism that contains all of the genetic material needed to develop into an adult human. Because abortion occurs well after fertilization, pro-life advocates believe that abortion ends a human life. Other targets of the pro-life movement are assisted-suicide laws and efforts by family members to withhold life support from the terminally ill or people who are in a persistent vegetative state (or "brain-dead").

While the pro-life movement remains solidly against abortion, its main cause, there has been some division among people in the movement over recent issues. One such issue is the "morning-after" pill, which can be taken after unprotected sex and works by preventing a fertilized egg from implanting in the uterus. Most pro-life advocates believe that because it acts after fertilization, it is a form of abortion and therefore murder. Some abortion opponents are not as strongly against the morning-after pill because it acts before the fertilized egg implants in the uterus, which many consider to be the time of conception, as opposed to fertilization.

Many pro-life advocates believe that embryonic stem cell research, whether the source of the stem cells is embryos created by the union of sperm and egg in vitro or through SCNT, is immoral. In each of the two alternative situations, harvesting the stem cells requires halting the development of a growing embryo, albeit at the earliest stages of its existence. However, to many people, this constitutes an act of murder.

## Embryonic stem cell research destroys human life.

At the center of the debate over embryonic stem cell research is the fundamental question "When does life begin?" The American public is bitterly divided over the answer to this question. For years, the question's main significance in public debate was in the debate over abortion. Most pro-life advocates believe that life begins when sperm and egg unite, resulting in a fertilized egg with a complete set of DNA and the potential, if nurtured in the uterus, to develop into a living person. Because abortion ends this potential life, abortion is morally wrong under that view. However, many supporters of abortion rights point to other times as the beginning of life, saying that abortion is permissible before that point.

Embryonic stem cell research is a much more recent controversy than abortion because stem cell technology did not develop until recent years. Therefore, the public debate on abortion that had been unfolding for decades has had a significant impact on the debate over embryonic stem cell research. Support or opposition to embryonic stem cell research typically corresponds to a person's position on abortion—abortion opponents also oppose embryonic stem cell research, while pro-choice advocates typically support (or at least do not oppose) embryonic stem cell research.

The belief—held by most within the pro-life movement—that life begins with the union of egg and sperm is the basis for most opposition to embryonic stem cell research. The President's Council on Bioethics described this position as follows:

> This view holds that only the very beginning of a new (embryonic) life can serve as a reasonable boundary line in according moral worth to a human organism, because it is the moment marked out by nature for the first visible appearance in the world of a new individual. Before fertilization, no new individual exists. After it, sperm and egg cells are gone—subsumed and transformed into a new, third entity capable of its own internally self-directed development. By itself, no sperm or egg has the potential to become an adult, but zygotes by their very nature do.[46]

As a result, people holding this belief refer to the embryo—from its earliest stage as a single-celled organism—as a human being or a person whose life should be protected. In a letter to U.S. senators, who were considering legislation reversing President Bush's stem cell funding policy, the National Right to Life Committee argued that such research destroys human life:

> Each human being begins as a human embryo, male or female. The government should not fund research that requires the killing of living members of the species Homo sapiens. [The bill under consideration] would require federal funding of research projects on stem cells taken from human embryos who are alive today, and who would be killed by the very act of removing their stem cells for the research. . . .[47]

To most pro-life advocates, there is no difference between destroying an early embryo with a few cells, as is done in embryonic stem cell research, and destroying a more fully developed embryo or fetus, as is done for an abortion. In the public debate, however, the distinction has been significant. In abortion debates, opponents frequently show photographs of aborted fetuses so as to highlight the developing human form. In contrast, the early-stage embryos destroyed for stem cell cultivation are visible only through a microscope and appear as a cluster of cells with no discernible human form.

Proponents of embryonic stem cell research have capitalized on this difference, convincing many people who oppose abortion to support embryonic stem cell research. Opponents frequently find themselves having to defend against two arguments made by research supporters. One argument is that embryos are destroyed at an early stage of their existence, before they develop certain human characteristics. Another argument is that the embryos are destroyed before they have been implanted in a woman's uterus and therefore are not developing as humans.

Addressing the first argument—the destruction of embryos at an early stage of their existence—Georgetown University professor Edmund Pellegrino (who would later become chair of the President's Council on Bioethics) testified to the National Bioethics Advisory Commission, rejecting "the idea that full moral status is conferred by degrees or is achieved at some arbitrary point in development."[48] He criticized researchers who approve of research up until the fourteenth day of development or some other point in the embryo's existence, saying, "Such arbitrariness is liable to definition more in accord with experimental need than ontological or biological reality."[49]

In other words, Pellegrino said that defining any time other than conception as the beginning of life is usually an attempt to justify something else. In the context of stem cell research, researchers seek to establish a time up until which destroying an embryo for stem cells is acceptable. Similarly, abortion supporters seek to define a point in development—such as viability, or when the developing fetus would be capable of living independently outside of the womb—until which abortion is acceptable.

However, Pellegrino testified, the pro-life movement rejects any distinct stages in the development of human life, holding to the belief that human development is a continuous process. He warned that making distinctions among different human lives can lead to unintended consequences:

> Terms such as "pre-embryo" or "pre-implantation embryo" seem to be contrivances rather than biological or ontological realities. Also rejected are socially constructed models that leave moral status to definition by social convention. In this view, moral status may be conferred at different times, or taken away, depending on social norms. This is a particularly perilous model for the most vulnerable among us: fetuses, embryos, the mentally retarded, or those in permanent vegetative states. The horrors of genocide in current events force us to recognize how distorted social convention can become, even in presumably civilized societies.[50]

British bioethicist Nigel Cameron testified before Congress in 2001 that settling the issue of the morality of stem cell research did not rely upon a strict definition of when life begins. He argued that even a more moderate view than one that life begins at conception supports a ban on embryonic stem cell research.

> I believe that we are losing sight of the middle ground. By that I mean that it is by no means necessary to take the view that the early embryo is a full human person in order to be convinced that deleterious experimentation is improper. There are many possible grounds for such a view—that we do not know if the embryo possesses full human dignity and should therefore be prudent; that the embryo possesses the potential to be a full human person and that such inbuilt potentiality entails profound respect, a view widely held and deeply threatened in this debate; or that membership in our species is enough to distinguish the human embryo from all other laboratory artifacts.[51]

In other words, he said, even if an embryo is viewed as a "potential" life rather than a life that has already begun, society should protect this potential life.

Opponents of embryonic stem cell research must also contend with the argument that human life does not begin until the fertilized egg is implanted in the womb and that embryos in vitro (in the laboratory or freezer) do not have moral standing as a human being. This is perhaps the more challenging argument facing opponents of embryonic stem cell research, because some powerful political figures who oppose abortion, including U.S. senators Orrin Hatch and Bill Frist, have endorsed it, breaking ranks with the pro-life movement.

In a report on human cloning, a majority of members of the President's Council on Bioethics rejected the argument that an embryo's presence in a laboratory dish diminished its humanity in any way. They instead endorsed a view that the embryo's identity was based on its genetic makeup rather than its environment, writing:

> The suggestion that extra-corporeal embryos are not yet individual human organisms-on-the-way, but rather special human cells that acquire only through implantation the potential to become individual human organisms-on-the-way, rests on a misunderstanding of the meaning and significance of potentiality. An embryo is, by definition and by its nature, potentially a fully developed human person; its potential for maturation is a characteristic it actually has, and from the start.[52]

The council members argued that an embryo's moral value should not be determined by its treatment by others—an embryo has no control over whether it is implanted in a woman's uterus or not. They drew a comparison to an animal living in captivity, arguing that it is no less a member of its species:

> The fact that embryos have been created outside their natural environment—which is to say, outside the woman's body—

and are therefore limited in their ability to realize their natural capacities, does not affect either the potential or the moral status of the beings themselves. A bird forced to live in a cage its entire life may never learn to fly. But this does not mean it is less of a bird, or that it lacks the immanent potentiality to fly on feathered wings. It means only that a caged bird—like an in vitro human embryo—has been deprived of its proper environment.[53]

The council members made it clear that there was nothing inherently immoral about creating an embryo in vitro but that people doing so must recognize that they are initiating a human life. They noted:

> There may, of course, be good human reasons to create embryos outside their natural environments—most obviously, to aid infertile couples. But doing so does not obliterate the moral status of the embryos themselves.[54]

However, proponents of embryonic stem cell research continue to argue that the early embryo is nothing more than a clump of cells, having more in common with a goldfish than with a human being. The answer to that argument, critics say, lies in the fact that the genetic information needed for the development of the embryo is contained in the embryo itself, rather than the woman in whose uterus it is implanted. Therefore, the identity of the embryo is independent of anyone else, and personhood exists prior to implantation. Testifying before Congress in 2001, Doerflinger of the U.S. Conference of Catholic Bishops argued:

> This view of the human embryo as a goldfish has apparently garnered support from some members of Congress who have generally opposed abortion. Their claim is that human life does not begin until placed in a mother's womb. Biologically, however, this is an absurd claim. An embryo's development is

directed completely from within—the womb simply provides a nurturing environment. Scientists tell us it would be technically possible to nurture a human embryo in a man's body by abdominal pregnancy, or in a mammal of another species, or even (someday) in an artificial womb. Upon being born could such a person morally be killed for his or her stem cells, because he or she never lived inside a woman's womb?[55]

## Research with "surplus" embryos is immoral.

Another tactic used by supporters of embryonic stem cell research is to say that destroying embryos for research purposes is acceptable as long as the embryos would have been destroyed anyway. This argument is made in reference to embryos that are initially created by couples seeking to conceive a child through IVF but are then donated by the couples for research purposes. Currently, there are estimated to be several hundred thousand embryos literally frozen in time: Because the IVF procedure is costly and implantation of the embryo is not always successful, fertility clinics create a large number of embryos for the couple at one time. The clinic then freezes the embryos, which can be thawed and implanted for multiple attempts at pregnancy. However, most couples either successfully become pregnant or give up before all the embryos are used, resulting in a large number of embryos being stored in a deep-freeze.

Many couples have decided to donate their unused embryos for research purposes. Although the federal government prohibits funding for research on stem cell lines developed after President Bush's announcement, researchers can legally develop stem cells with other types of funding. By convincing couples to donate frozen embryos, scientists can obtain embryos as a source of stem cells. The other option currently available to scientists is to create embryos in the laboratory by uniting sperm and egg through IVF, specifically for the purposes of stem cell research.

Many proponents of embryonic stem cell research have supported the former option—using embryos donated by couples who no longer want to use them to become pregnant. They argue that hundreds of thousands of these embryos exist, and that they will be destroyed anyway. Therefore, the argument goes, they should be used for the beneficial purpose of scientific research. However, the pro-life movement rejects any suggestion that the embryos remaining in the deep-freezers of fertility clinics are "surplus" embryos. Instead, they value these embryos as human life and oppose their destruction for stem cell research.

Many people support using embryos obtained in this way but oppose using IVF to create embryos specifically for research purposes. Opponents of embryonic stem cell research argue that this position reveals a weakness in the argument in favor

## THE LETTER OF THE LAW

### Louisiana Law Banning Embryo Research

*In general, state laws do not address embryonic stem cells by name; however, several states prohibit research using embryos, defined in a way that would include a prohibition on removing stem cells from an early embryo. For example, Louisiana law considers an embryo created by IVF that is viable—meaning either dividing in the laboratory or frozen to suspend cell division—to be a person with legal rights. It is not clear whether the law prohibits research on embryonic stem cell lines created outside of Louisiana.*

The use of a human ovum fertilized in vitro is solely for the support and contribution of the complete development of human in utero implantation. No in vitro fertilized human ovum will be farmed or cultured solely for research purposes or any other purposes. The sale of a human ovum, fertilized human ovum, or human embryo is expressly prohibited....

A viable in vitro fertilized human ovum is a juridical person which shall not be intentionally destroyed....

Source: Louisiana Revised Statutes, Title 9, Secs. 122, 129.

of destroying embryos for research purposes. As bioethicist Cameron points out:

> The widely held view that embryos should not be specially created for experimental purposes itself reveals a strong if undefined disposition to protect the embryo from abuse.[56]

Nevertheless, in 2001—before President Bush announced his guidelines on funding of stem cell research—the National Institutes of Health (NIH) proposed guidelines approving the funding of research conducted on stem cells derived from embryos donated by couples who had determined that they did not need the embryos for fertility purposes, but not on cells derived from embryos created for research purposes. These regulations were wiped out by President Bush's stem cell funding policy, but proponents of expanding embryonic stem cell research funding continue to use the "surplus embryo" argument.

Criticizing this position, Doerflinger argued that if the distinction between embryos created for reproduction and embryos created for research "is supposed to presuppose that [some] embryos really are human lives that deserve respect, it articulates a moral principle that is horrific for every patient subjected to human research"[57] because it establishes a hierarchy in which some lives are more valuable than others. This value system, in which lives that would be ended anyway could be ended sooner, he said, was contrary to established law:

> Currently we do not kill terminally ill patients for their organs, though they will die soon anyway, and federal law prohibits federally funded researchers from doing any harm to an unborn child slated for abortion, though that child will soon be discarded anyway.[58]

He also argued that approving of using unwanted embryos, on the basis that their parents would have discarded the embryos, neglected the duty of society to protect human life.

Drawing an analogy between discarding an embryo and child abuse, he argued:

> If parents were neglecting or abusing their child at a later stage, this would provide no justification whatever for the government to move in and help destroy the child for research material.[59]

In addition to the moral problems associated with designating some embryos as "surplus" and acceptable for destruction, Doerflinger disputed the factual basis of the argument, suggesting that discarding the embryos is not the only alternative to using them for research purposes. He testified:

> In any case, the claim that the embryos to be destroyed under the NIH guidelines will necessarily be destroyed anyway is actually a canard. That is not in the guidelines. It covers embryos found to be in excess of clinical need and the option of destroying them for their stem cells clearly stated should be offered as an option along side all the other options, including the option of adopting from another couple or saving for one's own later use.[60]

According to Doerflinger, the pro-embryonic stem cell research has repeatedly advanced a false argument (or "canard") that the embryos they wish to destroy would be destroyed anyway, when in fact a preferable alternative would be to convince the couples who created the embryos to either use them to get pregnant themselves or to donate them to an infertile couple.

## Many mainstream religions oppose embryonic stem cell research.

In spite of growing support for embryonic stem cell research, including support from many who consider themselves to be religious and attend worship services, mainstream religious groups have been leading the charge against embryonic stem cell research. Perhaps the most visible opposition has been that of the United States' largest single denomination, the Roman Catholic Church. With authority vested in the pope and a strict ruling structure including bishops who oversee many parishes in assigned geographic regions, the Church has presented an organized effort to limit embryonic stem cell research, even if many Catholics publicly or privately support such research.

Father Kevin Wildes of Georgetown University testified to the National Bioethics Advisory Committee that the Church's opposition was grounded in its desire to protect human life at all stages. He testified that the Church does not oppose biomedical research but that any research must be conducted only with the permission of the subject of the research and only if harm is minimized. With embryonic stem cell research, he testified, obtaining consent is impossible and the embryos are destroyed:

> Because the bishops work from an assumption that the human embryo should be treated as a human person, destruction of the embryo to conduct research is morally problematic. If one begins with this assumption, then many of our commonly held views on research ethics come into play. Research ethics are grounded in an understanding of respect for persons that views the consent of the research subject as essential to the moral appropriateness of the research itself. Furthermore, any research that is undertaken should minimize the risks and harms to research subjects. In research involving human stem cells, consent cannot be obtained, and it is certain that harm will come to the embryos because they must be destroyed so that the research might take place.[61]

As Father Wildes explained, the basis of the Roman Catholic Church's opposition to embryonic stem cell research is not that the stem cells are used in the laboratory in any particular way, but that researchers must find an alternative to destroying human embryos. He testified:

I do not think one can argue that there is, in Roman Catholic thought, opposition to stem cell research itself. The crucial moral issues and stumbling blocks are the problems of the derivation of the stem cells used in the research itself. That is, the destruction of embryos or the use of fetal tissue from abortion are the key moral problems. If you think that embryos should be treated as human persons, then it makes sense to argue that they should not be destroyed for purposes of research. However, if there were a way to conduct stem cell research without destroying human life, either embryonic or fetal, I do not think the Roman Catholic tradition would have a principled opposition to such research.[62]

Other religious groups share the Roman Catholic Church's opposition to embryonic stem cell research. Father Demetrios Demopulos of the Holy Trinity Greek Orthodox Church testified to the NBAC that the Greek Orthodox religion, along with Orthodox churches generally, opposes stem cell research. As he explained, the Orthodox Church believes that a human being, even at the earliest stage of development, is nonetheless a human being. In the Orthodox Church's view, even after birth, human beings are in a constant state of development:

Humans are created in the image and likeness of God and are unique in creation because they are psychosomatic, beings of both body and soul—physical and spiritual. We do not understand this mystery, which is analogous to that of the Theanthropic Christ, who at the same time is both God and a human being. We do know, however, that God intends for us to love him and grow in relationship to him and to others until we reach our goal of theosis, or deification, participation in the divine life through his grace. We grow in the image of God until we reach the likeness of God. Because we understand the human person as one who is in the image and likeness of God, and because of sin we must strive to attain that likeness, we can say that an authentic human person is one who is deified. Those of us who are still struggling toward theosis are human beings, but potential human persons.[63]

The Orthodox Church, Father Demopulos testified, does not draw a line (as proponents of embryonic stem cell research do) between those human beings who have already been born and those who are developing as embryos. In both cases, they are humans growing in the image of God: Even embryos at the earliest stage of development are, in Father Demopulos's words, striving for "authentic human personhood" just as those who have already been born. This quest begins whether the zygote is created through natural means or through IVF:

> We believe that this process toward authentic human personhood begins with the zygote. Whether created in situ or in vitro, a zygote is committed to a developmental course that will, with God's grace, ultimately lead to a human person. The embryo and the adult are both potential human persons, although in different stages of development. As a result, Orthodox Christians affirm the sanctity of human life at all stages of development. Unborn human life is entitled to the same protection and the same opportunity to grow in the image and likeness of God as are those already born.[64]

As a result, Father Demopulos testified, "the Orthodox Church promotes and encourages therapeutic advances in medicine and the research necessary to realize them, but not at the expense of human life."[65] His testimony supported searching other sources of stem cells and germ cells, such as adult stem cells and cells cultured from a fetus that has been spontaneously aborted, meaning that the mother had had a miscarriage.

Although many Protestant religious groups have a less centralized governing structure and therefore leave more room for varying opinions, mainline Protestant religions have also voiced their opposition to embryonic stem cell research. In testimony before the NBAC, Professor Gilbert Meilaender, Jr., of Valparaiso University, noted the difficulty of characterizing the viewpoints of Protestant religions. However, he testified that he would attempt to generalize from a variety of viewpoints and found a general opposition to embryonic stem cell research:

> I cannot claim to speak for Protestants generally—alas, no one can. I will, however, try to draw on several theologians who speak from within different strands of Protestantism. I think you can and should assume that a significant number of my co-religionists more or less agree with the points I will make. You can, of course, also assume that other Protestants would disagree, even though I like to think that, were they to ponder these matters long enough, they would not.[66]

Meilaender quoted three theologians to illustrate three major points in opposition to embryonic stem cell research. For his first point, he quoted Reformed Calvinist theologian Karl Barth, who had written, "No community, whether family, village or state, is really strong if it will not carry its weak and even its very weakest members."[67] In Meilaender's view, allowing exploitation of the weakest members of society—whom he identifies as embryos—is inconsistent with traditional Christian thought on the concept of "personhood," which holds that a person is not a person by accomplishment or attaining certain abilities but merely by coming into being:

> We have become accustomed in recent years to distinguishing between persons and human beings, to thinking about personhood as something added to the existence of a living human being—and then to debating where to locate the time when such personhood is added. There is, however, a much older concept of the person—for which no threshold of capacities is required—that was deeply influential in Western history and that had its roots in some of the most central Christian affirmations.[68]

For his second point, Meilaender quoted Mennonite theologian John Howard Yoder, who warned against seeking easy solutions, which sometimes can lead to poor decisions:

> None of us should pretend to be indifferent to attempts to relieve or cure heart disease, Parkinson's and Alzheimer's diseases, or diabetes. [However,] we may sometimes need to deny ourselves the handiest means to an undeniably good end. In this case, the desired means will surely involve the creation of embryos for research—and then their destruction. The human will, seeing a desired end, takes control, subjecting to its desire even the living human organism. We need to ask ourselves whether this is a road we really want to travel to the very end.[69]

Meilaender's third point, which he supported by quoting Methodist theologian Stanley Hauerwas, was that a church community should speak truthfully. In the context of stem cell research, Meilaender testified:

> I have in mind matters such as the following: that we avoid sophistic distinctions between funding research on embryonic stem cells and funding the procurement of those cells from embryos; that we not deceive ourselves by supposing that we will use only "excess" embryos from infertility treatments, having in those treatments created far more embryos than are actually needed; that we speak simply of embryos, not of the "pre-embryo" or the "pre-implantation embryo" (which is really the unimplanted embryo); and that, if we forge ahead with embryonic stem cell research, we simply scrap the language of "respect" or "profound respect" for those embryos that we create and discard according to our purposes. Such language does not train us to think seriously about the choices we are making, and it is, in any case, not likely to be believed. You can help us to think and speak truthfully, and that would be a very great service indeed.[70]

In other words, Meilaender accuses proponents of embryonic stem cell research of deception and hypocrisy. First, he critiques the idea that conducting research with embryonic stem cells that have already been derived is somehow on a higher moral ground than the process of obtaining those cells from embryos—the distinction that seems to have led to the Bush policy on funding embryonic stem cell research. Second, Meilaender dismisses the idea that embryos created by IVF but not implanted for birth are "excess" embryos rather than human beings. Third, he rejects distinctions frequently made between embryos prior to their fourteenth day of development and those after that stage, criticizing the use of the term "pre-embryo" to describe the embryo in its earliest stage because even at that early stage it is an embryo. Fourth, he criticizes the distinction between an embryo that is frozen or exists in a laboratory and one that has been implanted or formed in utero. Some pro-life proponents of embryonic stem cell research, such as Senator Orrin Hatch, have made this distinction to justify support for stem cell research but opposition to abortion. Finally, Meilaender believes that for researchers to say that they are proceeding with "respect" for embryos used in embryonic stem cell research is hypocritical, as the embryos are destroyed in the process. In Meilaender's view, the religious beliefs of Protestants compel them to seek truth, and much of the support for embryonic stem cell research is based on lies or distortions.

## The potential for cures does not justify destroying embryos.

Proponents of embryonic stem cell research often use a Machiavellian ("the end justifies the means") argument in favor of embryonic stem cell research: Even if destroying embryos might not be the best thing to do, they say, the benefit is enormous. They list the diseases for which embryonic stem cells are thought to provide hope—including diabetes, heart disease, Parkinson's disease—and say that the potential to cure these diseases in people who have already been born justifies the destruction of an embryo in its earliest stages.

Opponents reject this argument, maintaining that even if embryonic stem cell research held great promise—which is debatable—this promise would not justify the destruction of embryos. As Doerflinger explained:

> In our view, human life deserves full respect and protection at every stage and in every condition. The intrinsic wrong of destroying innocent human life cannot be "outweighed" by any material advantage—in other words, the end does not justify an immoral means.[71]

Anton-Lewis Usala, a medical researcher who has suffered from type-1 diabetes since infancy, testified before a Senate committee that emotional appeals from people suffering from illnesses cloud the issue that human life must be destroyed in order to pursue embryonic stem cell research. He said:

> It is not honest to bring before this committee people such as myself, who have chronic illnesses for which there is no cure, as a valid argument for funding human embryonic stem cell research. There are many alternative paths, and if there is a legal or ethical reason not to conduct this research, public resources can be all the more effectively focused on those alternative paths.[72]

Usala noted that acceptance of the argument that the potential benefit of embryonic stem cell research justified the destruction of embryos would lead to dire consequences for American society:

> In my view, the United States is a uniquely just society, being the first government in the history of humankind where the rights of the individual supersede the perceived right of the state. This is the foundation that was established by the first 10 amendments to our Constitution. Should human embryonic stem cell research be funded, it will be the first time

in U.S. history the federal government has determined the best "use" for a human being. This would be a cataclysmic paradigm shift. The perceived right of the state will have superseded the right of the individual. Even during the horrific times of slavery, the federal government did not fund programs using human beings for state purposes (although clearly individuals did).[73]

Doerflinger also predicted dire consequences for justifying the destruction of human embryos by touting the potential benefit to others:

Acceptance of a purely utilitarian argument for mistreating human life would endanger anyone and everyone who may be very young, very old, very disabled, or otherwise very marginalized in our society.[74]

A "utilitarian" philosophy includes the theory that society should seek to do what provides the most benefit to the most people, which in this case, Doerflinger argues, would result in ignoring the rights of the few.

In his testimony to NBAC, Father Demopulos explained that the potential for cures promised by supporters of embryonic stem cell research is not a factor in determining whether or not embryonic stem cell research is moral. Even in the face of proof that embryonic stem cells can cure disease, the benefit to other people would not, he testified, justify the destruction of human embryos to cure disease in others. Father Demopulos acknowledged that "the Orthodox Church has a long tradition of encouraging the 'medical art' that alleviates unnecessary pain and suffering and restores health."[75] Nevertheless, as fallible human beings, he testified, researchers cannot morally make the decision to relieve unnecessary pain and suffering in some people by sacrificing others, as would be the case if human embryos were destroyed in order to help cure people with chronic disease. As he noted, "The Church, however, also has reminded us that this art is given to us by God to be used according to his will, not our own."[76]

Daniel Callahan of the Hastings Center suggested an alternative argument as to why the search for medical cures does not justify the destruction of embryos. He suggested that opponents of embryonic stem cell research "challenge directly the notion that there is an obligation to carry out a war against disease. There are plenty of good spending alternatives available to improve our common life."[77] For the billions that the state of California has promised for embryonic stem cell research, he suggested that a better use would be a campaign to eliminate illiteracy.

## Summary

A significant percentage of the American population comes from religious traditions that view life, from the moment sperm fertilizes egg, as inviolable. The pro-life movement, with some dissenters, opposes embryonic stem cell research because it destroys human embryos. Even if so-called "surplus" embryos are used exclusively, and no matter what the potential benefit, the moral objections stand.

# Embryonic Stem Cell Research Is Compatible with Contemporary Moral Standards

It is a story that is repeated all too often. A young child develops unusual behaviors. He is always thirsty, drinks water and juice constantly, and goes to the bathroom nonstop. Thinking something is strange but not overly concerned, the child's parents bring him to the pediatrician and ask about the child's behavior. A quick prick of the finger, a test with a blood glucose meter available at any drug store, and the stunning news is delivered to the child's parents: He has type-1 diabetes. For the rest of his life, he will have to take insulin shots multiple times per day, watch what he eats, and monitor his blood sugar every few hours. With diligence, he can lessen his chances of blindness, losing a limb, or needing a kidney transplant. However, his diabetes will be with him every day for the rest of his life.

According to the Juvenile Diabetes Research Foundation (JDRF), each day 35 children in the United States are diagnosed with type-1 diabetes, and the organization is dedicated to finding a cure. Although there has been some success with a technique of transplanting cells taken from the pancreas of an organ donor, this technique has been performed only about 250 times since its inception in the year 2000—far short of the needs of the up to 3 million Americans with diabetes. JDRF continues to fund many types of research, but its leadership is particularly excited by the potential of embryonic stem cell research to finally lead to a cure.

Many people believe that society has a moral duty to do everything possible to help cure disease. Conditions such as diabetes, heart disease, spinal cord injuries, Parkinson's disease, Alzheimer's disease, and others take an enormous toll on society, both in causing death and affecting quality of life. A growing number of Americans support embryonic stem cell research. Some believe that destroying embryos consisting of only a handful of cells cannot be considered taking human life. Many people belong to religious traditions that, unlike the Catholic Church, do not consider fertilization to be the beginning of a human life. Other people have some moral hesitation but support using the hundreds of thousands of embryos frozen in fertility clinics, reasoning that the embryos would otherwise be allowed to perish. To many people, the potential cures are simply too compelling to avoid experimenting with embryos.

## Using early embryos for stem cell research does not take human life.

Even at a time when abortion foes are gathering their troops to mount a challenge to the legality of abortion, embryonic stem cell research is finding support, including among those who oppose abortion. Proponents of research have generally been successful in trying to distance embryonic stem cell research from the abortion debate. Senator Patty Murray's comments, made in a hearing about stem cell funding, are typical:

> This is not about abortion. Stem cells are not a result of abortions. It is not about destroying life. It is about improving life

and in many cases saving lives. Federal support of stem cell research does not legitimize abortion. It does not reduce the value of all human life. But it does give us a promising new avenue for research that I believe could save many lives.[78]

Many proponents, in fact, try to win support among the pro-life movement by characterizing embryonic stem cell research as pro-life. At the same hearing, James West, founder of the Geron Corporation, which funded some of the earliest embryonic stem cell research, prefaced his remarks by referring to his own history of opposition to abortion:

It may be useful to point out that I think of myself as pro-life in that I have an enormous respect for the value of the individual human life. Indeed, in my years following college I protested abortion clinics. My goal was not to say to women that they did not have the right to choose. My intent was simply to urge them to reconsider the destruction of a developing human being. [80]

He then argued that his support for embryonic stem cell research was consistent with his pro-life beliefs:

Despite my strong convictions about the value of the individual human life, in 1995 I organized the collaboration between Geron Corporation and the laboratories of Dr. James Thomson and John Gearhart to isolate human embryonic stem cells and germ cells from living human embryos and fetuses. My reasons were simple. These technologies are entirely designed to alleviate human suffering and to save human life. They are, in fact, pro-life. The opponents that argue they destroy human lives are simply and tragically mistaken.[80]

Though many within the pro-life movement believe that life begins with the union of sperm and egg and should be inviolable from that moment forward, research supporters have won a number of abortion foes by using a number of arguments. Two are aimed at dividing the loyalties of those who view abortion as ending a human life. The first argument is that embryonic stem cell research, because it uses embryos at a very early stage of development, is more acceptable, morally speaking, than aborting an embryo or fetus at a later stage of development. The second argument makes a distinction between embryos developing in utero and embryos created in vitro but not yet implanted.

The pro-life movement generally supports the view that human life begins with the union of sperm and egg. Under this view, timing is irrelevant to the morality of destroying an embryo or fetus. The destruction of an embryo moments after fertilization is no more acceptable morally than having an abortion in the eighth month of pregnancy. However, not all opponents of abortion hold this view. Some people point to some time after fertilization as the point after which abortion is morally unacceptable, and supporters of embryonic stem cell research have used these differences in viewpoint to help generate support for harvesting stem cells, which typically takes place before the embryo reaches its fourteenth day of development.

These views, as the President's Council noted, depend on an "implicit or explicit claim regarding the importance of a particular feature, capacity, form, or function (or the progressive accumulation of these) in defining a developing organism as meaningfully a member of the human race."[81] In other words, views that accommodate the destruction of embryos generally hold that either a physical development or the ability to perform some function gives the embryo a greater moral status, or at least more strongly identifies the embryo as a "person" rather than a "clump of cells."

Some hold that destruction of the embryo is acceptable up until the point at which it acquires human form. As the President's Council noted:

> Some observers also argue that certain rudimentary features of the human form must be apparent before we can consider

a human embryo deserving of protection. In this view, the human form truly signals the presence of a human life in the making and calls upon our moral sentiments to treat the being in question as "one of us." Different versions of this argument appeal to different particular elements (or combinations of elements) of the human form as decisive, but all suggest that a "ball of cells" is not recognizably human and therefore ought not to be treated as simply one of us.[82]

Another argument based on the form of the embryo is an argument that the development of the nervous system marks the time at which the embryo deserves protection:

Many observers regard the nervous system as an especially important marker of humanity, both because the human brain is critical for all "higher" human activities, and because the nervous system is the seat of sensation and, especially relevant to this case, the sensation of pain.[83]

Prior to the development of the ability to think or feel pain, the argument goes, the destruction of the embryo does not pose the same problems as destroying an embryo or fetus capable of sensation or feeling pain.

Another landmark in the developmental process is the appearance of the "primitive streak" at about the fourteenth day of development. In the context of the embryonic stem cell debate, supporters have generally focused their efforts on convincing people that destroying embryos prior to the development of the primitive streak is morally acceptable. This view supports the advancement of embryonic stem cell research, as stem cells are typically harvested before this stage. Proponents try to portray the embryo at this stage as a "clump of cells."

Research proponents also justify harvesting stem cells from embryos in the pre-primitive streak phase by pointing out that "twinning" can still occur at this stage. Supporters of the position that life begins at fertilization frequently point out that all of the genetic information needed for development is present in the fertilized egg. However, proponents of research question whether individual identity can be traced prior to the development of the primitive streak because—up until that time—the embryo may divide, forming "identical" twins. Although "identical" twins share the same DNA, and often many other characteristics, they are indisputably different individuals. Additionally, although such an occurrence is extremely rare, two early-stage embryos can join together to form a "chimera," or one individual with two sets of DNA. To West, the belief that an individual person exists prior to the development of the primitive streak is incompatible with the possibility of these biological occurrences. He testified:

> These and other simple lessons in embryology teach us that despite the dogmatic assertions of some theologians, the evidence is decisive in support of the position that an individual human life, as opposed to merely cellular life, begins with the primitive streak, (i.e., after 14 days of development). Otherwise we are left with the logical absurdity of ascribing to the blastocyst personhood when we know, scientifically speaking, that no individual exists (i.e., the blastocyst may still form identical twins).[84]

In an article for the *Albany Law Review*, Roman Catholic priest and bioethics professor James McCarthy—noting that the Church had traditionally based its position on the beginning of life on current understandings of science—argued that the Church should "reflect on its own rich tradition in dealing with personhood and individuation" and consider whether "a zygote or developing embryo should be revered and respected, is not an individual of the human species with rights" because of the possibility of twinning or the formation of a chimera.[85]

Supporters of embryonic stem cell research have pressed hard for public support of the position that destruction of the embryo prior the development of the primitive streak is not the moral equivalent of taking a human life. By arguing for this position, they leave room for harvesting stem cells, which takes place prior to the fourteenth day, while distancing themselves from the abortion debate, which involves embryos and fetuses much further along the path of development. Research proponents have had some success with this approach, if public support for embryonic stem cell research is any indication.

Arguments marking some point of development as the beginning of life (or "personhood") are often met with counterarguments that if we cannot determine for certain when life begins, we should err on the side of preserving life. However, some proponents of stem cell research believe that the development of the primitive streak is a significant enough event that it is possible that human life as we know it does not begin before this development. West argued that biology provides a definitive answer that human life does not begin before the development of the primitive streak. He testified:

> Indeed, early in my life I might have argued that since we don't know when a human life begins, it is best not to tamper with the early embryo. But, with time I learned the facts of human embryology and cell biology. . . . [It] is absolutely a matter of life and death that policy-makers in the United States carefully study the facts of human embryology and stem cells. A child's understanding of human reproduction could lead to disastrous consequences.[86]

While acknowledging that a great difference of opinion exists about whether an early-stage embryo is a life deserving legal protections, West attributed the disagreements to a lack of understanding of the biological concepts that he had outlined. He testified:

> I would argue that the lack of consensus is driven by a lack of widespread knowledge of the facts regarding the origins of human life on a cellular level and human life on a

# Stem-cell work may bypass objections

Studies show the possibility of collecting stem cells without destroying viable human embryos. The proposals might overcome religious objections and allow federal funding for promising research.

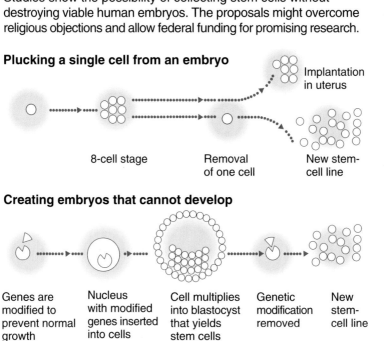

**Plucking a single cell from an embryo**

Implantation in uterus

8-cell stage

Removal of one cell

New stem-cell line

**Creating embryos that cannot develop**

Genes are modified to prevent normal growth

Nucleus with modified genes inserted into cells

Cell multiplies into blastocyst that yields stem cells

Genetic modification removed

New stem-cell line

One of the main objections to the use of embryonic stem cells for research is that doing so requires the destruction of the embryo, and hence—if one believes that life starts at conception—the destruction of life. Scientists are working on ways to extract stem cells either from embryos that never will be viable, or in such a way that it will not destroy the embryo, as illustrated above.

somatic and individual level. So the question of when does life begin is better phrased "When does an individual human life begin?"[87]

West accused opponents of using religious belief to hinder the progress of science, drawing an analogy to the Roman

Catholic Church's persecution of seventeeth-century astronomer Galileo Galilei:

> Some dogmatic individuals claim, with the same certainty the Church opposed Galileo's claim that the earth is not the center of the universe, that an individual human life begins with the fertilization of the egg cell by the sperm cell. Like previous vacuous pronouncements, this is simply not based in fact or, for that matter, without basis in religious tradition.[88]

The second major argument advanced by supporters of embryonic stem cell research to help win abortion opponents to their cause is that embryos in vitro are morally different from embryos that have already implanted in a woman's uterus. Senator Orrin Hatch, a longtime abortion opponent, summarized his position:

> While I understand that many in the pro-life community will disagree with me, I believe that a human life, a human's life, begins in the womb, not in a petri dish or a refrigerator.[89]

The argument regarding implantation in the uterus—which in nature happens at around the same time as the development of the primitive streak—as an important benchmark in the beginning of life seems to rest on several assumptions. First, the laboratory environment is portrayed as artificial and not a part of "natural" life. Second, it is pointed out that an embryo can only develop for so long in the laboratory environment—until about the fourteenth day. Finally, existence prior to implantation in the uterus is perilous, West notes:

> It is estimated that approximately 40 percent of preimplantation embryos formed following normal human sexual reproduction fail to attach to the uterus and are simply destroyed as a result.[90]

## Using surplus embryos in stem cell research is an acceptable approach.

Although many supporters of embryonic stem cell research do not see the early-stage embryo as a human life, and therefore do not have a moral objection to using it as a source of stem cells, they understand that many people have some moral qualms about this position. Perhaps as a fallback position, many people have advocated policies approving of the use of the estimated 400,000 embryos created through IVF by infertile couples but no longer wanted for the purposes of giving birth. These people suggest that embryos are entitled to some form of respect but make a practical argument that embryos unwanted by infertile couples are destined to be destroyed anyway, therefore destroying them in a way that benefits others is preferable to simply discarding them.

Orrin Hatch, the anti-abortion U.S. senator who supports embryonic stem cell research, has argued that the numbers simply do not work in favor of those who say that embryos should be adopted rather than destroyed. With hundreds of thousands of embryos frozen in fertility clinics, finding enough willing surrogate mothers would be a significant task. Additionally, each of the couples who created the frozen embryos would have to consent to the adoption process. As a result, said Hatch:

> It is inevitable that extra embryos are created, embryos that simply will not be implanted in a mother's womb. As these embryos sit frozen in a test tube, outside the womb, under today's technology, there is no chance for them to develop into a person.
>
> While I have no objection to considering ways to foster adoption of embryos, there are a host of issues associated with this which must be worked out. And while those issues are being considered, the reality today is that each year thousands, and I am told the number may be tens of thousands, of embryos are routinely destroyed. Why shouldn't

these embryos slated for destruction be used for the good of mankind?[91]

Father McCartney came to a similar conclusion in his law review article:

> The lesser of the two evils is the one that accords more respect for human life understood generically, i.e., the option that at least allows the genome to continue to live as a tissue culture of stem cells, not the one that allows death by thawing.[92]

Many appear persuaded by this argument. In fact, the National Institutes of Health at one point proposed regulations that would have allowed research on embryos that would otherwise be discarded—regulations wiped out by President Bush's limits on embryonic stem cell funding. James Childress, a professor of religious ethics and biomedical ethics, testified that limiting research to surplus embryos would allow embryonic stem cell research to continue, without the progress of the research leading to the destruction of embryos. He testified to Congress:

> This prospective policy can be undertaken without sanctioning or encouraging further destruction of human embryos. Those were legitimate, major concerns in President Bush's statement. We can establish effective ethical safeguards to ensure that a couple's voluntary decision to destroy their embryos is voluntary and informed, or that their decision to donate them for research is voluntary, informed, and uncompensated. The research, then, would only determine how the destruction occurs, not whether it will occur.[93]

In other words, the total number of embryos that are destroyed is determined by the couples who created the embryos. Regardless of whether embryonic stem cell research is conducted with the discarded embryos, the number of embryos destroyed remains the same. Since the announcement of the Bush funding policy, couples have donated surplus embryos for the purpose of harvesting stem cells, but none of these stem cells can be researched using federal funding.

## Many mainstream religions support embryonic stem cell research.

One of the major criticisms of embryonic stem cell research is that it conflicts with the widely held religious beliefs of Americans. Much of the battle against funding and in favor of bans has been led by religious organizations, notably the Roman Catholic Church but also loosely affiliated groups of conservative Protestants. However, religious opposition to stem cell research among the United States' major religious groups is far from uniform. Some mainstream religious groups find nothing in embryonic stem cell research that conflicts with their moral laws, and in fact, some groups argue that because embryonic stem cell research holds such potential to cure deadly and disabling diseases, conducting such research amounts to a moral duty.

In testimony to the National Bioethics Advisory Commission in 2000, a number of religious leaders expressed the support of their denominations for embryonic stem cell research. These leaders represented a diversity of viewpoints, including Jewish, Muslim, and Christian.

Ronald Cole-Turner of the Pittsburgh Theological Seminary testified about the United Church of Christ's support of embryonic stem cell research. The church, frequently associated with liberal causes and support of low-income groups, had released a pro-embryonic-stem-cell-research policy statement in 1997, when such research was in its earliest stages. The policy adopted by the church supported research on embryos until the fourteenth day of development. Cole-Turner testified that the United Church of Christ supported federal funding for research on embryonic stem cells.

Cole-Turner noted that the church's support of research was subject to certain conditions, and he called on the commission to ensure that safeguards were in place to guarantee that research be conducted ethically. The first condition was that research be conducted only if "a clear and attainable benefit for science and for medicine [were] indicated in advance," a condition that he believes had been met by current researchers: "It is reasonable to think that now, with pluripotent stem cell technology, such benefit is becoming clearer."[94] The second condition was that widespread public discussion should precede embryonic stem cell research, and as Cole-Turner explained:

> We stipulate this condition for two reasons. First, we believe that although enormous advances for medicine lie ahead in these areas of research and that we are obliged to work to achieve these advances, our efforts could be undermined, and it could be very bad for science if research proceeds in the short term without broad public understanding and support. Public misunderstanding and public exclusion from discussion could result in public rejection of this and related forms of research.
>
> The second reason why we set forth the condition of advanced public discussion and support is that we value living in a society that makes basic public moral decisions based on the deliberations of informed citizens. As a historic church, our congregational forebears extended congregational decision-making to the public square. As a church today, we believe that our views are not the only views worth hearing but that public policy on morally problematic issues should be the result of honest and sustained discourse during which all views are brought forward in public. This view of a public society is an article of faith with us.[95]

Several Jewish theologians testified to the NBAC that Jewish law does not prohibit embryonic stem cell research. Rabbi Elliot Dorff of the University of Judaism noted that Jewish law, in contrast to Roman Catholic doctrine, makes distinctions among embryos based on their stage of development and whether the embryo is developing in vitro (in the laboratory) or in utero (in the womb):

> Stem cells for research purposes also can be procured from donated sperm and eggs mixed together and cultured in a petri dish. Genetic materials outside the uterus have no legal status in Jewish law, for they are not even a part of a human being until implanted in a woman's womb, and even then, during the first 40 days of gestation, their status is "as if they were simply water." Abortion is still prohibited during that time, except for therapeutic purposes, for in the uterus such gametes have the potential of growing into a human being. Outside the womb, however, at least at this time, they have no such potential. As a result, frozen embryos may be discarded or used for reasonable purposes and so may the stem cells that are procured from them.[96]

Note that in his testimony, Rabbi Dorff seems to indicate three categories of embryos: (1) embryos developing in utero after 40 days of gestation; (2) embryos developing in utero in the first 40 days of gestation; and (3) embryos developing in vitro. Embryos in the first category have the greatest status, while those in the third category—embryos developing in vitro—have no status under Jewish law. Another Jewish theologian, Rabbi Moshe D. Tendler of Yeshiva University, testified that before the fortieth day of gestation, the embryo had the same moral status as sperm or an unfertilized egg: "Such an embryo has the same moral status as male and female gametes, and its destruction prior to implantation is of the same moral import as the 'wasting of human seed.' "[97]

By contrast, Rabbi Dorff testified, people suffering from chronic diseases are entitled to the best care possible:

> Our bodies belong to God; we have them on loan during our lease on life. God, as owner of our bodies, can and does

impose conditions on our use of our bodies. Among those conditions is the requirement that we seek to preserve our lives and our health.[98]

Because of that duty, he argued, scientists should seek whatever means are at their disposal, including embryonic stem cell research, in order to cure disease:

> The Jewish tradition accepts both natural and artificial means for overcoming illness. Physicians are the agents and partners of God in the ongoing act of healing. Thus, the mere fact that human beings created a specific therapy rather than finding it in nature does not impugn its legitimacy. On the contrary, we have a duty to God to develop and use any therapies that can aid us in taking care of our bodies, which ultimately belong to God.[99]

In his testimony, Rabbi Tendler warned that efforts by religious groups to block embryonic stem cell research based on their own religious beliefs pose a risk of harm to those who do not share those religious beliefs. He testified:

> Surely our tradition respects the effort of the Vatican and fundamentalist Christian faiths to erect fences that will protect the biblical prohibition against abortion. But a fence that prevents the cure of fatal diseases must not be erected, for then the loss is greater than the benefit. In the Judeo-biblical legislative tradition, a fence that causes pain and suffering is dismantled. Even biblical law is superseded by the duty to save lives, except for the three cardinal sins of adultery, idolatry, and murder.
>
> The commendable effort of the Catholic citizens of our country to influence legislation that will assist in preventing the further fraying of the moral fabric of our society must not impinge on the religious rights and obligations of others. Separation of church and state is the safeguard of minority rights in our magnificent democracy. Life-saving abortion is a

categorical imperative in Jewish biblical law. Mastery of nature for the benefit of those suffering from vital organ failure is an obligation. Human embryonic stem cell research holds that promise.[100]

# Stem Cell Research Enhancement Act of 2005

*This bill, which was passed by the House of Representatives but not the Senate, is one of several bills that have attempted to extend funding of embryonic stem cell research beyond what has been allowed by President Bush.*

(a) In General—Notwithstanding any other provision of law (including any regulation or guidance), the Secretary shall conduct and support research that utilizes human embryonic stem cells in accordance with this section (regardless of the date on which the stem cells were derived from a human embryo).

(b) Ethical Requirements—Human embryonic stem cells shall be eligible for use in any research conducted or supported by the Secretary if the cells meet each of the following:

(1) The stem cells were derived from human embryos that have been donated from in vitro fertilization clinics, were created for the purposes of fertility treatment, and were in excess of the clinical need of the individuals seeking such treatment.

(2) Prior to the consideration of embryo donation and through consultation with the individuals seeking fertility treatment, it was determined that the embryos would never be implanted in a woman and would otherwise be discarded.

(3) The individuals seeking fertility treatment donated the embryos with written informed consent and without receiving any financial or other inducements to make the donation.

Source: H.R. 810 (109th Congress, 1st session).

## The benefit to the suffering justifies destruction of early-stage embryos.

Many people frame the argument in favor of embryonic stem cell research in terms of relative benefit and harm. Early on during the Congressional stem cell debate, Senator Bill Frist encouraged his colleagues to think about the number of embryos that would have to be destroyed in the name of stem cell research, saying that the number of embryos destroyed would be small in relation to the number of people helped.

> The really exciting thing about embryonic stem cells, it is not sort of a one for one. It is not like that you have to take a blastocyst, which is really 20 to 30 inner cells coupled with an outer supportive framework . . . [to] help one research project and then take another one to help another research project or another. The great power and potential—again, it is unpredictable—of these is the fact that these will perpetuate themselves forever and that once you take a cell line, that cell line you can grow, and you can grow it in an identical fashion and share with researchers all over the world, as long as [there is] informed consent. That is the real power. . . . [101]

In Frist's opinion, opponents of embryonic stem cell research are dishonestly arguing that funding embryonic stem cell research will create an enormous demand for embryos:

> I think that is an important concept because people have in their image that all these embryos are going to be created and they are living and there is going to be destruction of these embryos that is going to go on millions and millions and thousands of times. It is just important for people to understand you do not need unlimited cell lines. Exactly how many I think it is worth talking to the scientists about. [102]

Others have warned that the moral objections to embryonic stem cell research is reminiscent of previous moral objections to fields of study that have saved lives and helped many live healthier lives. Fischbach and Fischbach note that important technologies such as IVF and organ transplants "were once thought to be too dangerous or were seen as 'playing God.'"[103] They also mention the controversy surrounding recombinant DNA, which involves placing human genetic material into bacteria. Addressing Congress, Irv Weissman also cited the recombinant DNA debate as an example of how moral objections can stand in the way of life-saving research. He pointed out that when first discovered, the technique was highly controversial:

> In the late 1970s, and early 1980s, the Cambridge, Mass., city council and the Berkeley, CA, city council considered prohibiting recombinant DNA research in their jurisdictions, and the issue of safety was raised in the U.S. Congress. Recombinant DNA is spliced together DNA segments, and the issue at that time was putting human genes like insulin into bacteria to produce human insulin for diabetics. Many thought such genetic manipulations could be dangerous, and others wished it banned because it offended them or because they reserved to God the right to "create life." [104]

Weissman argued that the federal government took the correct approach to recombinant DNA technology—to regulate it rather than to ban it. By establishing ethical standards for recombinant DNA research, the government had enabled researchers to make great strides while preventing any moral disaster:

> But instead of banning the research, the NIH regulated such research. Even today, to carry out a recombinant DNA experiment with new methods or possibly dangerous genes it is required to seek and obtain approval from these regulatory bodies. What was the result? Only the birth of biotechnology, the expansion of these research techniques to every branch of biomedical research, and the annual saving or making better of [greater than] 100,000 lives per year.[105]

The alternative, banning recombinant DNA research, would have been immoral, Weissman suggested:

> Had this recombinant DNA research been banned, those lives would be saddled with disease or lost. The lost or impaired lives of those people would, in my view, be the moral responsibility of those who advocated or helped enact the ban.[106]

Advocates like Weissman think that opponents of embryonic stem cell research would have similar moral responsibility for standing in the way of cures that might be developed as a result of stem cell research.

—————————•————————•——————•—————————

## Summary

A significant number of Americans, including some who oppose abortion, have begun to support embryonic stem cell research. To many, the early-stage embryo used to cultivate stem cells is not morally equivalent to a living person or even an older embryo or fetus. Some pro-life politicians have said that before an embryo is implanted in the womb, it does not have the same moral standing, while others make the argument that hundreds of thousands of embryos will simply perish at fertility clinics and they might as well be put to good use. Even if the usefulness of embryonic stem cells has not been established, the need to cure disease justifies experimentation with embryos, they say.

# Cloning for Any Purpose Is Immoral

Dolly the sheep died in 2003 at the relatively early age of six. Normally, the death of a sheep does not make international headlines, but Dolly was no ordinary sheep. Dolly was the first mammal "cloned" from an adult mammal. Ian Wilmut's team of scientists in Scotland made an exact genetic copy of an adult female sheep. It is not accurate to call this sheep Dolly's "mother," because Dolly has no father. The scientists had taken the nucleus (inner contents) of one of this sheep's mammary (breast) cells and injected it into an egg cell, which had been taken from a second female sheep and had its nucleus removed. The resulting cell was then stimulated with electricity to induce it to start dividing, and finally it was implanted into the uterus of a third female sheep. After her birth, the scientists confirmed that all of Dolly's genes came from the first female sheep, unlike natural offspring, which have one set of genes from the father and one from the mother.

Dolly's birth had sent shockwaves through the world, and her death raised further questions. Many people are gravely concerned about the idea of producing human clones. They point to Dolly's health problems and say that human clones would not be healthy and could perhaps contaminate the "gene pool." On a moral level, they question whether cloning is playing God and worry that clones would be considered second-class humans.

No reputable scientists are talking about using Wilmut's techniques—somatic cell nuclear transfer (SCNT)—to produce human babies. However, many people are excited about using the techniques to produce cloned embryos solely for the purpose of culturing stem cells from these embryos in the early days of their existence. In 2005, it appeared that a team of Korean scientists had successfully used SCNT to create human embryonic stem cells; it turns out, however, that the research had been faked.

Although human cloning has not been achieved, the pro-life movement wants to stop it from ever happening. The pro-life movement, while opposing all forms of embryonic stem cell research, is particularly concerned with research on cloned embryos. The pro-life movement usually talks about "cloning" rather than the more harmless-sounding SCNT. The use of the term "cloning" generates opposition to the process, as the public has a negative feeling about the idea: Opinion polls have revealed that only 38 percent of Americans support "cloning" embryos for research, while 72 percent support using "somatic cell nuclear transfer" to create embryos for research.[107] The simple change in phrasing, though having the same meaning, can have a major impact on public perception.

Proponents of embryonic stem cell research try to defuse the negative connotations of the word "cloning" by referring to two types of cloning, "reproductive cloning" and "therapeutic cloning." The former refers to using SCNT to create an embryo that will be implanted into a woman's uterus for the purposes of her giving birth to a human genetically identical to the person cloned. The latter term refers to using SCNT to create an embryo that will be used as a source of embryonic stem cells, thereby destroying the embryo and preventing the birth of a genetically identical human. Making this distinction allows proponents of embryonic stem cell research to denounce reproductive cloning while supporting therapeutic cloning.

To date, federal law has been silent on the issue of the legality of cloning, although like other forms of embryonic stem cell research, federal funds would not be available for the study of embryonic stem cells created by SCNT, as they did not

## Wisconsin's Vetoed Anti-Cloning Law

*In 2005, the Wisconsin legislature approved a sweeping anti-cloning law, which would have outlawed cloning for any purpose, including performing SCNT for the purposes of stem cell research. The state has been a leader in stem cell research, and the governor vetoed the bill before it could become law.*

(1) In this section:

(a) "Asexual reproduction" means reproduction not initiated by the union of an oocyte and a sperm.

(b) "Enucleated oocyte" means a fertilized or unfertilized oocyte, the nuclear material of which has been removed or inactivated.

(c) "Human cloning" means asexual reproduction accomplished by introducing nuclear material from one or more human somatic cells into an enucleated oocyte so as to produce a living organism having genetic material that is virtually identical to the genetic material of an existing or previously existing human organism.

(d) "Human embryo" means a human organism derived by fertilization, parthenogenesis, cloning, or any other means from one or more human gametes or human diploid cells. "Human embryo" includes a zygote but does not include a human organism at or beyond the stage of development at exist when President Bush formulated his policy. Several state legislatures have taken up the issue, with mixed results. Indiana, for example, banned cloning in 2005; on the other hand, in Wisconsin, the governor vetoed an anti-cloning law.

Opponents of embryonic stem cell research have numerous objections to stem cell research using SCNT. First, they reject the distinction between reproductive and therapeutic cloning, noting that the same process (SCNT) is used, whether the claimed purpose is doing research or cloning humans for live birth. Second, they believe that the process of human cloning

which the major body structures are present.

(e) "Human parthenogenesis" means the process of manipulating the genetic material of a human oocyte, without introducing into the oocyte the genetic material from any other cell, in a way that causes the oocyte to become a human embryo.

(f) "Living organism" includes a human embryo.

(g) "Somatic cell" means a cell that has a complete set of chromosomes and that is obtained or derived from a living or dead human organism at any stage of development.

(2) No person may knowingly do any of the following:

(a) Perform or attempt to perform human cloning or human parthenogenesis.

(b) Transfer or acquire for any purpose a human embryo produced by human cloning or human parthenogenesis or any embryo, cell, tissue, or product derived from a human embryo produced by human cloning or human parthenogenesis.

(3) (a) Any person who violates sub. (2) is guilty of a Class G felony....

Source: Wisc. Assembly Bill 499 (2005) (not enacted).

itself is an immoral transgression into the course of nature. Third, they believe that even though cloning is immoral, killing cloned embryos is no more morally acceptable than killing other embryos. Finally, they fear that allowing SCNT technology to develop opens the door for its abuse.

## "Therapeutic cloning" is not a separate procedure.

Supporters of the use of SCNT for stem cell research have tried to clearly distinguish "good cloning" from "bad cloning" by arguing that the use of SCNT for the purposes of research—what they call "therapeutic cloning"—is acceptable while the use of SCNT to create exact genetic copies of existing people—what they call "reproductive cloning" is unacceptable. Opponents of cloning say, however, that this distinction is misleading because the process of creating the embryo through SCNT is the same regardless of its purpose. In other words, a scientist attempting to create an embryo with the intention of destroying it to obtain its stem cells would go through the exact same procedures in the laboratory as a scientist attempting to create an embryo that could be implanted into a woman's uterus, resulting in a live birth.

In a press release while the Wisconsin legislature was considering a bill criminalizing cloning—regardless of its purpose—the organization Wisconsin Right to Life argued:

> There is no scientific difference between any cloned embryos and there are not two types of cloning. That is a fallacy created by the supporters of human cloning.
>
> The only difference is the purpose for which a cloned embryo has been created. All cloned embryos are created in exactly the same way and whether they were created to be implanted into a woman's body or to be destroyed in medical experiments, they are genetically the same.[108]

The organization was responding to lobbying efforts by supporters of embryonic stem cell research who were trying to amend the law so that it would permit "therapeutic cloning"—an amendment that the pro-life forces referred to as the "clone and kill amendment"[109] because it would permit SCNT so long as the embryo was destroyed for research purposes.

Wisconsin Right to Life accused "reproductive cloning" supporters of wrongfully assigning a lesser moral value to embryos created for research:

> Supporters of human cloning would have lawmakers and the public believe that the embryos cloned for research are somehow "different" than other cloned embryos in order to make it more palatable to advocate their destruction in medical experiments. It is also important to note that the terms "therapeutic" and "reproductive" cloning were coined by the supporters of human cloning. There is nothing "therapeutic" about it for the embryo who is destroyed![110]

State legislatures have rejected the distinction between "reproductive" and "therapeutic" cloning. The Wisconsin legislature approved the anti-cloning bill without the "clone and kill" amendment; however, the anti-cloning bill did not become law because the governor vetoed it. The anti-stem-cell law enacted that same year in nearby Indiana, however, outlawed "cloning," which it defined as "use of asexual reproduction to create or grow a human embryo from a single cell or cells of a genetically identical human."[111] Under this definition, SCNT is illegal. The vetoed Wisconsin law was more specific, defining cloning as:

> Asexual reproduction accomplished by introducing nuclear material from one or more human somatic cells into an enucleated oocyte so as to produce a living organism having genetic material that is virtually identical to the genetic material of an existing or previously existing human organism.[112]

Indiana law took a firmer stance against SCNT than federal law, which has been silent on the legality of the procedure. In February 2003, the U.S. House of Representatives passed by a wide margin a bill that would have outlawed human cloning via SCNT for any purpose, whether for reproduction or for biomedical research. A bill, however, must be passed by both the House of Representatives and the Senate and approved by the president (in most cases) in order to become law. Despite the widespread support in the House of Representatives and President George W. Bush's expressed opposition to human cloning, anti-cloning laws have stalled out in the Senate.

The President's Council on Bioethics advises the president on matters of bioethics, including stem cell research and cloning. In 2002, they issued a report in which a majority of the council expressed support for federal restrictions on the use of SCNT for embryonic stem cell research, concluding:

> A permanent ban on cloning-to-produce-children coupled with a four-year moratorium on cloning-for-biomedical-research would be the best way for our society to express its firm position on the former, and to engage in a properly informed and open democratic deliberation on the latter.[113]

Because the council was divided on the issue of "cloning-for-biomedical-research"—as opposed to "cloning-to-produce-children," which it unanimously opposed—the report contained both majority and minority opinions about the ethics of using SCNT as a source of embryos for stem cell research. In the majority opinion, the participating council members outlined a number of arguments against the practice. Although the recommendations are not legally binding, they provide a number of arguments in favor of banning cloning, including the use of SCNT for research purposes. Among the objections were that the process of cloning humans through asexual reproduction is itself morally objectionable, and that embryos created by SCNT deserve the same protection from destruction as embryos created by IVF.

## The process of cloning is immoral, regardless of intent.

Regardless of opinion on whether therapeutic and reproductive cloning can be distinguished from one another, many people think that the act of cloning—creating an embryo with the genetic material of an existing person rather than by uniting the genetic material of a man and a woman—is itself immoral, regardless of its purpose. The majority of the President's Council wrote that the first cloning of a human being would be a monumental event in human history, possibly altering the course of the development of the human species:

> It is worth noting that human cloning—including cloning-for-biomedical-research itself and not simply cloning-to-produce-children—would cross a natural boundary between sexual and asexual reproduction, reducing the likelihood that we could either retrace our steps or keep from taking further steps. [114]

In other words, once scientists started down that path, it would be hard to turn back. The first embryo created by SCNT—whether for research purposes or for reproductive purposes—would be uniquely subject to the power of a human creator, they charged:

> Cloning-for-biomedical-research and cloning-to-produce-children both begin with the same act of cloning: the production of a human embryo that is genetically virtually identical to its progenitor. The cloned embryo would therefore be the first human organism with a single genetic "parent" and, equally important, with a genetic constitution that is known

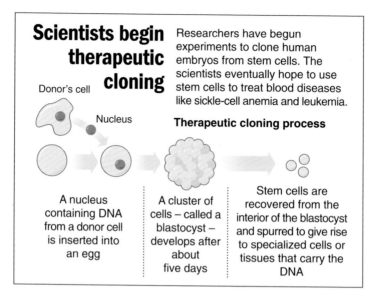

# Scientists begin therapeutic cloning

Researchers have begun experiments to clone human embryos from stem cells. The scientists eventually hope to use stem cells to treat blood diseases like sickle-cell anemia and leukemia.

Donor's cell

Nucleus

**Therapeutic cloning process**

A nucleus containing DNA from a donor cell is inserted into an egg

A cluster of cells – called a blastocyst – develops after about five days

Stem cells are recovered from the interior of the blastocyst and spurred to give rise to specialized cells or tissues that carry the DNA

**The graphic above illustrates the process by which scientists hope to clone human embryos from stem cells. Some people believe that creating an embryo from the genetic material of an individual, rather than through the sexual union of a man and a woman, is itself immoral.**

and selected in advance. Both uses of cloning mark a significant leap in human power and human control over our genetic origins. Both involve deliberate genetic manipulation of nascent human life.[115]

The opinion of this group of council members reflects an ongoing concern shared by many, including mainstream religious groups. Although the Roman Catholic Church has taken a strong stand against "therapeutic cloning," based on its opposition to the destruction of human embryos, another basis for the Church's objection to all forms of cloning is that humans, rather than God, would have control over the form of the offspring. At a U.N. hearing, Monsignor Renato Martino testified:

The act of cloning is a predetermined act which forces the image and likeness of the donor and is actually a form of imposing dominion over another human being which denies the human dignity of the child and makes him or her a slave to the will of others. The child would be seen as an object and a product of one's fancy rather than as a unique human being, equal in dignity to those who "created" him or her. The practice of cloning would usurp the role of creator and would thus be seen as an offense before God.[116]

Some critics of cloning also think that the process exploits women. In a U.S. Senate hearing about the impact of cloning on women, Andrew Kimbrell, executive director of the International Center for Technology Assessment in Washington, D.C., listed several reasons to support this contention. First, donating the eggs needed for cloning is a risky procedure that involves taking medication to stimulate production of eggs and undergoing surgery to "harvest" the eggs. The same process is used by women seeking to conceive a child; however, critics like Kimbrell distinguish harvesting eggs for cloning as an unacceptable risk because so many eggs would be needed to pursue stem cell research. He testified:

Research cloning is a highly inefficient process, which would require an unlimited supply of human eggs. It has been estimated that research cloning might be able to provide up to 1.7 million therapies per year. Assuming a highly optimistic success rate of one stem cell culture per five cloned embryos, and one cloned embryo per 10 eggs, these therapies would require 85 million eggs, or 8.5 million egg donors.[117]

The result of this demand, he suggested, would be "an explosion in demand for human eggs," which in turn, he testified:

would exacerbate the coercive nature of the lucrative egg donation industry. Currently, compensation to women for egg "donation" is uncapped and ranges from an average payment of $5,000–$6,000 to as high as $80,000. The increase in egg demand created by research cloning is likely to increase the price of eggs and coercive potential of the egg market. The burden of egg supply will likely fall on underprivileged women.[118]

## Cloned embryos are no less deserving of respect than those created by other means.

While sharing an opposition to reproductive cloning, the two sides of the stem cell debate take a different view of what the moral status of a cloned human embryo would be. To proponents of research, the cloned human embryo poses no threat to society or the human race so long as it is not allowed to live to term. In other words, killing a cloned embryo prevents a moral evil. However, people taking a pro-life position believe that to kill a cloned embryo would itself be morally wrong and that to prevent that wrong from taking place, therapeutic cloning must be banned.

In its campaign for the state's anti-cloning law, Wisconsin Right to Life argued that proponents of stem cell research were, by using the term "therapeutic cloning," trying to imply that embryos created by SCNT were somehow less than human, a contention they rejected:

> In fact, [embryos created by SCNT] are genetically the same as embryos in IVF clinics and embryos created with the union of a man and woman. In other words, an embryo is an embryo is an embryo.[119]

If someone were to successfully conduct SCNT using a human egg cell and human genetic material, the resulting embryo—though created in a way much different from the union of sperm and egg—would be biologically very similar or indistinguishable in form. In criticizing therapeutic cloning, the majority group of the President's Council argued that the similarity in form was more important that the difference in process in assigning moral value to the cloned embryo:

> That the embryo in question is produced by cloning and not by the fertilization of an egg should not, in our view, lead us to treat it differently. The cloned embryo is different in its origins, but not in its possible destiny, from a normal embryo. Were it brought to term it too would indisputably be a member of the human species. We caution against defining the cloned embryo into a "non-embryo"—especially when science provides no warrant for doing so.[120]

If anything, the majority argued, the process by which cloned embryos are created call for even greater safeguards to their existence. Dismissing arguments that cloning embryos for destruction was no different from using embryos initially created by IVF for implantation by infertile couples, the majority of the council wrote:

> Those who minimize or deny this distinction—between producing embryos hoping that one of them will become a child and producing embryos so that they can be used (and destroyed) in research—demonstrate the very problem we are worried about. Having become comfortable with seeing embryos as a means to noble ends (be it having a child or conducting biomedical research), they have lost sight of the fact that the embryos that we create as potential children are not means at all. Even those who remain agnostic about whether the human embryo is fully one of us should see the ways in which conducting such research would make us a different society: less humble toward that which we cannot fully

understand, less willing to extend the boundaries of human respect ever outward, and more willing to transgress moral boundaries that we have, ourselves, so recently established, once it appears to be in our own interests to do so. We find it disquieting, even somewhat ignoble, to treat what are in fact seeds of the next generation as mere raw material for satisfying the needs of our own.[121]

This desire to use the "seeds of the next generation" as "raw material" for research, the majority wrote, belies researchers' promise of "respect" for cloned embryos—meaning that they would limit the use of cloning to legitimate research projects for serious conditions. The majority responded:

We do not understand what it means to claim that one is treating cloned embryos with special respect when one decides to create them intentionally for research that necessarily leads to their destruction. This respect is allegedly demonstrated by limiting such research—and therefore limiting the numbers of embryos that may be created, used, and destroyed—to only the most serious purposes: namely, scientific investigations that hold out the potential for curing diseases or relieving suffering. But this self-limitation shows only that our purposes are steadfastly high-minded; it does not show that the means of pursuing these purposes are respectful of the cloned embryos that are necessarily violated, exploited, and destroyed in the process. To the contrary, a true respect for a being would nurture and encourage it toward its own flourishing.[122]

In the end, the majority suggested, therapeutic cloning is inconsistent with a belief in fundamental principles of equality:

If we add to this description a commitment to equal treatment—the moral principle that every human life deserves our equal respect—we begin to see how difficult it must be to suggest that a human embryo, even in its most undeveloped and germinal stage, could simply be used for the good of others and then destroyed. Justifying our intention of using (and destroying) human embryos for the purpose of bio-medical research would force us either to ignore the truth of our own continuing personal histories from their beginning in embryonic life or to weaken the commitment to human equality that has been so slowly and laboriously developed in our cultural history.[123]

## Allowing SCNT technology to develop creates the potential for its abuse.

In Greek mythology, Pandora lived at a time when everything on Earth was peaceful. Pandora's husband warned her not to open a box that had been a gift from Zeus, the king of the gods. Pandora's curiosity got the better of her, however, and when she opened the box, all of the evils that had been stored in the box were released into the world, leading to war, famine, and other evils. Opponents of cloning believe that to allow cloning for any reason, even a limited reason such as stem cell research, would amount to opening Pandora's box. As the majority of the President's Council warned, support for therapeutic cloning "ignores the hazardous moral precedent that the routinized creation, use, and destruction of nascent human life would establish for other areas of scientific research and social life."[124]

One such danger is "organ farming"—raising a cloned embryo to the point that an organ may be surgically removed for transplantation into the cloned human. With organ trans-plantation, an ever-present danger is the body's rejection of foreign cells, necessitating a lifetime of drugs that suppress the immune system, preventing rejection of the organ but making a person much more prone to develop infections. With a cloned organ, it is speculated, a transplant might be done without risk of rejection. The majority of the President's Council warned that acceptance of cloning for stem cell research opens the door to organ farming:

> Today, the demand is for stem cells; tomorrow it may be for embryonic and fetal organs. The recent experiments with cloned cow embryos implanted in a cow's uterus already suggest that there may be greater therapeutic potential using differentiated tissues (for example, kidney primordia) harvested from early fetuses than using undifferentiated stem cells taken from the very early embryo. Should this prove to be the case, pressure will increase to grow cloned human blastocysts to later stages—either in the uteruses of suitably prepared animal hosts or (eventually) using artificial placentalike structures in the laboratory—in order to obtain the more useful tissues. One can even imagine without difficulty how a mother might be willing to receive into her womb as a temporary resident the embryonic clone of her desperately ill child, in order to harvest for that child life-saving organs or tissues.[125]

Another danger is the possibility of using SCNT to create "chimeras," or a cross between species (this is distinct from a naturally occurring chimera, which is an organism with two sets of genes, both sets from the same species). One of the problems with pursuing SCNT on a large scale is that it relies on a large source of human eggs, which are "hollowed out" for implantation with genetic material. Obtaining egg donations involves costs, risks, and ethical dilemmas. Some worry that researchers will bypass this problem by implanting human genetic material into egg cells obtained from other species. The majority group on the council warned:

> Experiments creating animal-human hybrid-embryos, produced by inserting human DNA into enucleated rabbit oocytes, have already been conducted in China, with

development up to the blastocyst stage. Yet far from solving our ethical dilemma, the use of animal eggs raises new concerns about animal-human hybrids. We have no idea where these and later interspecies experiments might lead. Yet the creation of such chimeras, even in embryonic form, shows how ready we seem to be to blur further the boundary—biological and moral—between human being and animal.[126]

Although proponents of cloning argue that fears of organ farming and human-animal chimeras are far-fetched, Charles Krauthammer believes that once given approval for cloning, scientists would quickly argue for approval of organ farming. The reason, he suggests, is simple: It would have a much better chance of producing cures. He asks rhetorically why scientists would go through the trouble of harvesting cells from the blastocyst, growing stem cells in the laboratory, and coaxing them into producing the necessary cells: "Why not let the blastocyst grow into a fetus that possesses the kinds of differentiated tissue that we could then use for curing the donor?"[127]

## Summary

Even though a human being has never been cloned, mammals have been, and that's close enough to scare the pro-life movement, which has been working for bans on cloning at the state, federal, and international levels. Whether the purpose is cloning to make babies or to harvest stem cells, opponents say, cloning is simply wrong. The process of creating life outside of the union of sperm and egg is a violation of the laws of nature, many think, and to create life simply to destroy it for research creates its own problems.

# Using SCNT to Create Embryos for Stem Cell Research Is Morally Acceptable

In May 2005, Korean scientist Hwang Woo Suk published a paper in a prestigious scientific journal highlighting his laboratory's cultivation of stem cell lines from embryos created by somatic cell nuclear transfer (SCNT), or what many people refer to as "cloning" because the process involves transferring a living person's DNA into a hollowed-out egg cell, resulting in an exact genetic copy of the cloned person. This research was the first time that the technique that had been used to create Dolly the sheep had been used for human reproduction—or so it seemed. Before the year was out, the research had been proven to have been a fraud, Hwang Woo Suk was disgraced, and the promising Korean stem cell industry was left in disarray.

The exposure of the fraud generated mixed reactions throughout the world. Although pro-life opponents of cloning took a breath of relief, many proponents of embryonic stem cell research were disappointed. They view SCNT as a promising technique that could add a new dimension to embryonic stem cell research.

Proponents of using SCNT for embryonic stem cell research often refer to the (as-yet-unproven) technique as "therapeutic cloning" to distinguish it from "reproductive cloning," or using the technique to produce babies. Though pro-life opponents say cloning is cloning, supporters say that legitimate scientists have no interest in reproductive cloning and that banning reproductive cloning can be achieved while leaving the door open to therapeutic cloning. Proponents of such research do not see a moral problem with either the process of cloning an embryo in the laboratory or destroying it to harvest stem cells. They also believe that cloned embryos will provide a superior source of embryonic stem cells for many applications, suggesting that having one's own laboratory-cloned cells could help cure disease without being rejected by the immune system. Although the technique remains a future goal, proponents are already fighting against bans.

## Therapeutic and reproductive cloning are legitimately distinguished.

While opponents of using SCNT to create human embryos generally refer to the process as "cloning," which stirs up negative thoughts among the public, supporters tend to use the scientific term SCNT, or the phrase "therapeutic cloning" to describe what they propose to do—transfer human genetic material into the outer membrane of a donated human egg, resulting in an mbryo on which research could be conducted.

Supporters of SCNT also believe, however, that the use of the term "therapeutic cloning" is a legitimate attempt to convey what is done with SCNT and why scientists do it—sending a clear message that they have no interest in "reproductive cloning. As Paul Berg of Stanford University testified before Congress:

## How cloning works

An egg's nucleus is removed and replaced with DNA from the cell of the animal to be cloned.

Inside the egg, cells prepare to multiply as chromosomes duplicate themselves.

**Egg**

**Chromosomes**

# Tiny proteins block cloning capabilities

Scientists haven't been able to clone monkeys like they can clone barnyard animals. Now they've discovered why: proteins removed in the cloning process cause a chromosomal mismatch.

## What goes wrong

When the nucleus is removed from a monkey egg, motor proteins cling to it and are also removed. That doesn't happen when cloning non-primates.

**Motor proteins** in the egg help form zipper-like spindles that the chromosomes use to align. Once in place, the spindles help pull the cell into two identical parts.

**Spindle**

Spindles don't form correctly.

**Misaligned Chromosomes**

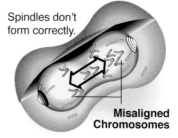

Cells continue to divide until the embryo is ready to plant into a surrogate mother.

Cells divide, but abnormal chromosomes can cause defects and affect the pregnancy.

**Healthy, developing embryo**

**Abnormal cells in egg**

The graphic above illustrates the process of cloning on the left. While this process has been successful in cloning certain animals, such as Dolly the sheep, the same process has been unsuccessful when applied to monkey eggs, as show on the right.

The term 'cloning', before it was tainted by attributing nefarious purposes to it, is a legitimate scientific term to describe the preparation of an 'infinite' number of copies of, for example, a single molecule, a cell, a virus or a bacterium. . . . In short, cloning is not a dirty word! We must not allow the term to be hijacked to frighten the public and to cloud the issues that confront us.[128]

What matters, supporters say, is not the procedure used to create the embryo but the intention with which it is created. In his personal statement attached to the President's Council's report on cloning, council member Michael Gazzaniga wrote:

In juxtaposition to cloning-to-produce-children is cloning-for-biomedical-research. This is another matter entirely. Cloning-for-biomedical-research is carried out with a completely different set of intentions from cloning-to-produce children. Cloning-for-biomedical-research is a bit of a misnomer, but it is the term the panel wants to use instead of "therapeutic cloning," for it is meant to cover not only cloning for therapeutics (for such diseases as diabetes, Parkinson's disease, and so on) but also that cloning now deemed necessary for understanding all genetic disorders. This is cloning for the sole purpose of enabling various types of lifesaving biomedical research. Perhaps the Council should have called it "lifesaving cloning."[129]

The members of the President's Council who supported the use of SCNT to create embryos for research pointed to a list of serious diseases for which SCNT might someday provide cures and listed several types of research and therapies that could be done with embryos produced by SCNT but could not be done with embryos created by IVF. Among the diseases and conditions highlighted by the council members were type-1 (or juvenile) diabetes, Parkinson's disease, Alzheimer's disease, spinal cord injuries, heart disease, and amyotrophic lateral sclerosis (ALS, or Lou Gehrig's disease).

The first promising use of SCNT is to create human models to study the development of disease. In order to treat and develop cures for diseases, scientists must be able to figure out how the disease develops. SCNT holds special promise for the study of genetic diseases. Every person has "genes" encoded into our complex DNA molecules—areas of our DNA that gives all of us our similarities as humans. However, genes take multiple forms, called alleles, which make us all individuals. Sometimes, a genetic mutation, or change in form, occurs to the DNA, which can either be harmless or lead to serious consequences, such as cancer. Certain alleles and mutations are associated with diseases, which are consequently referred to as genetic diseases.

With genetic disease, the presence of an allele or mutation in a person's DNA leads to some result in the body that causes the disease. Parkinson's disease, which affects the nervous system, leading to shaking and loss of muscular control, is associated with at least two specific gene mutations. These mutations are associated with the collection of a specific type of protein in the brain cells of people who have Parkinson's disease. Scientists might be able to develop better means of detecting or treating Parkinson's disease if they knew how exactly the genetic mutations led to the collection of this protein in the brain cells. One option for studying the process is to isolate the human genes associated with Parkinson's disease and inject them into animals, so that the gene integrates with the animal's DNA. As the council members pointed out, however, "to study human disease, it is generally preferable to work with human cells and tissues," because the animal models do not exactly recreate the human disease process, and therefore a complete understanding cannot be gained.[130]

As described by the council members, here is how the process would work: Scientists would first perform SCNT, taking genetic material from cells donated by people who had

Parkinson's disease and implanting this material into donated human egg membranes. They would then take the embryonic stem cells from these embryos and manipulate them to create the type of brain cells affected by Parkinson's disease—recall that stem cells have the ability to form many types of human cells. The council members argued:

> A preferable alternative to introducing mutant [human] genes into normal [animal] cells is to begin with human cells that are already abnormal—in this case, cells carrying the mutant genes that predispose their bearers to Parkinson's disease....These cells would provide a vastly improved model for understanding the metabolism of [the protein] and its role in the development of Parkinson's disease.[131]

The second use highlighted by the council members was using cloned cells to test new drug therapies. They suggested that the same process of creating embryonic stem cells that replicate the brain cells of people with Parkinson's disease, and which accumulate the protein implicated in the disease, would be useful in testing new drugs. Drugs that prevented the accumulation of the protein in the cells being studied in the laboratory could be pursued further as a possible treatment for Parkinson's disease.

The third use was to create immune-compatible cells and tissues for individual recipients, which the council members suggested might be an advantage that cloned embryonic stem cells have over those cultured from embryos created by IVF. Perhaps the greatest hope for stem cells is that cells injected into a person suffering from a medical condition can lead to the regeneration of tissue: Injecting spinal cord cells can lead to regeneration of the spine after an injury, or injecting heart cells can lead to the regeneration of a diseased heart. The problem of the body's immune system attacking these cells, however, remains a problem for cells created with another person's DNA—as would be the case with cells grown from stem cells originally cultured from embryos created by IVF. However, with a heart or spinal nerve cell cultured from a cloned embryo—it is hoped—the body's immune system would not recognize the cell as foreign and would therefore not attack it.

Finally, the council members suggested that SCNT could be used to create genetically modified cells for people with genetic diseases, or "gene therapy." They theorized that scientists could extract the genetic material of a person suffering from a particular genetic disease, "repair" the DNA by replacing the defective gene, and use it to culture stem cells that could then be injected back into the person, for example, creating bone marrow cells for someone with an immune disease.

## SCNT is a scientific advance, not a transgression of nature.

Supporters of SCNT reject the idea that by bypassing the traditional method of creating an embryo—uniting sperm from one individual and the egg of another—a moral line is being crossed. Rather than viewing SCNT as humans crossing into the realm of God, supporters tend to view SCNT as a logical progression in developing medical technology. While admitting that using SCNT for the purpose of reproduction might cause some moral objections, they do not think that the process itself poses moral difficulties and that when used for research purposes, the process is scientifically and morally valid.

Testifying before the Senate Judiciary Committee, Thomas Murray, president of the Hastings Center, acknowledged that scientists must follow some sort of moral code so as to avoid past atrocities such as when Nazi scientists conducted cruel "experiments" or when people were allowed to suffer from syphilis without being informed of their condition. However, he distinguished human cloning from such cruelty, arguing that because the moral question was not clearly settled against therapeutic cloning, scientific progress should not be halted:

Americans value the quest for new frontiers; today's explorers are more likely to wear white coats and inhabit laboratories than to paddle canoes or hike over mountain passes. Scientific inquiry is obliged to respect moral limits. That principle was resoundingly affirmed in the trials at Nuremburg and in our own nation's apology to the subjects of the Tuskegee syphilis study. But when we have no consensus that a form of research is ethically improper, the wiser course is to allow people to follow their individual consciences. This respects the value of freedom of inquiry without forcing people to violate their beliefs.[132]

Many supporters of embryonic stem cell research view SCNT not as an act of creation wrongfully taken from the hands of God but as nothing more than a scientific procedure. As Michael Gazzaniga wrote in his personal statement attached to the President's Council's cloning report:

> Scientists prefer to call this somatic cell nuclear transfer for a simple reason. That is all it is. Any cell from an adult can be placed in an egg whose own nucleus has been removed and given a jolt of electricity. This all takes place in a lab dish, and the hope is that this transfer will allow the adult cell to be reprogrammed so that it will form a clump of approximately 150 cells called a blastocyst. That clump of cells will then be harvested for the stem cells the clump contains, and medical science will move forward.[133]

In fact, the members of the President's Council who supported using SCNT for biomedical research suggested that, although the moral questions are not easily resolved, scientists might even have a moral obligation to take advantage of the opportunities offered by stem cell research on embryos created by SCNT:

American society and human communities in general have an obligation to try to heal the sick and relieve their suffering. This obligation, deeply rooted in the moral teaching of "love of neighbor," lies heaviest on physicians and health-care professionals who attend to individual patients. But it guides also the activities of biomedical scientists and biotechnologists whose pioneering research and discoveries provide new and better means of healing and relieving those who suffer. Research on cloned human embryos is one more path to discovering such means.[134]

## Embryos created by SCNT do not deserve legal protections.

Supporters of using SCNT to create embryos for stem cell research vary on their stance on the moral value of the embryos created by SCNT but feel that the embryos do not deserve legal protection from being used for research. In the President's Council's report on cloning, some of the commissioners who supported reproductive cloning acknowledged that the embryo created by SCNT had moral standing as a potential human being, much like an embryo created by IVF. They noted, "Embryos have a developing and intermediate moral worth, such that the early human embryo has a moral status somewhere between that of ordinary human cells and that of a full human person."[135] Nevertheless, they concluded, "We also hold that the embryo can be used for life-saving or potentially life-saving research while still being accorded the 'special respect' it deserves. . . ."[136]

A few of the council members supporting reproductive cloning, however, declared, "We accord no special moral status to the early-stage cloned embryo. . . ."[137] In their view, embryos created by SCNT had no greater value than the somatic cells (the cells that make up the body) from which they were created. A frequent argument made against the destruction of early-stage embryos is that they have the potential to develop into living people and therefore they should be treated as individual people. The dissenting council members, however, argued:

> Thanks to the results of nuclear transplantation research, there is reason to believe that every human cell has the genetic potential to develop into a complete human being, if used in cloning efforts to produce a child. If mere potentiality to develop into a human being is enough to make something morally human, then every human cell has a special or inviolable moral status, a view that is patently absurd.[138]

Their argument relies on the following reasoning. If, as suggested by pro-life advocates, an embryo must be treated as a person because it has the potential to develop into a person, then every cell in the human body must be treated as an individual person because every cell in the liver, skin, blood, etc., has the potential to develop into a human if used in SCNT.

Some supporters of using SCNT for stem cell research make a biological distinction between the embryos created by SCNT and those created by IVF or natural conception. Testifying before Congress in 2005, Rudolf Jaenisch, professor of biology at the Massachusetts Institute of Technology, noted the general failure of animal cloning experiments to produce healthy offspring. Noting that human cloning promised even less chance of success for producing healthy human babies, he argued that cloned early-stage embryos (blastocysts) are not the functional equivalent of those created by the union of sperm and egg because they do not "represent potential normal human life."[139] He testified:

> From all experience with cloned animals, I would argue that the cloned blastocyst has little, if any, potential to ever develop into a normal baby. Most will die in development and the few that survive to birth will develop severe defects with age because of the reprogramming faults following nuclear transplantation. . . .

Because a cloned blastocyst is so different from the normal blastocyst which is derived from a fertilized egg . . . it should not be designated as an embryo.[140]

Proponents of using SCNT for stem cell research argue that the focus of protections must be the women who donate the eggs that are used for implantation with genetic material, as well as people who donate somatic cells for the collection of genetic material. In developing guidelines for research funded by Proposition 71, California's massive stem cell initiative, the California Institute for Regenerative Medicine placed restrictions on the way stem cells and donated cells could be used as well as restrictions on how such materials were collected.

The California regulations have two main thrusts, both of which focus on protection of the living people who donated cells for research rather than these cells or any embryos created in the process. The first major concern is informed consent, which in medical research typically refers to ensuring that a patient fully understands the risks and benefits (if any) of the research in which he or she is participating. For example, researchers studying an experimental drug would be required to prove that people taking the drug knew that the drug had not been proven effective in treating a condition and that side effects were possible. In the context of donating eggs or other cells for use in SCNT, California requires that researchers inform donors about how their genetic materials will be used, including ensuring that the donors know that embryos may be destroyed, that cells might be implanted into other people, and that the products created might be patented for the researchers' financial gain. Additionally, the regulations require researchers to inform donors that their efforts cannot be guaranteed to provide a benefit to others: Though stem cell research has great promise, many experiments are destined to fail.

The other major focus of the California regulations is protecting women from exploitation or harm. Donating eggs is a risky procedure that involves both surgery and taking drugs that stimulate ovulation—getting the ovaries to release more eggs than would be released normally in the reproductive cycle. Among the risks is a risk to the woman's future ability to conceive children. Because of the risks, California wanted to prevent researchers from taking advantage of poor women, who might be more tempted to donate eggs for money. Therefore, the regulations ban paying women for their eggs. At the same time, the state wanted to protect women who voluntarily donate their eggs for the public good. The regulations thus require researchers to pay for donors' medical expenses, including covering any medical costs relating to any complications from the donation process, such as treating infections or corrective surgery.

## Protections can easily be put into place to prevent reproductive cloning.

Supporters of SCNT for research purposes find themselves defending the procedure against "slippery slope" arguments— meaning that if we as a society allow therapeutic cloning, then we will inevitably allow reproductive cloning. Some opponents fear that allowing SCNT technology to develop will allow it to be misused for reproductive cloning and therefore believe any use of SCNT must be banned. Supporters of therapeutic cloning, however, argue that the line between therapeutic and reproductive cloning is easily maintained.

Former NIH director Harold Varmus testified before Congress against a bill that would have outlawed any form of cloning. Varmus made several points. First, if experience with animal cloning is any indication, it will be much more difficult to produce a cloned embryo capable of surviving to birth than it will be to create an embryo that can survive 14 days to the blastocyst stage. He said supporters of the total cloning ban had "obscured the profound differences between studies of immature human cells in a culture dish and the full process required to make a cloned human being."[141]

Second, Varmus said, it was easy to identify and criminalize the behavior that would differentiate therapeutic and reproductive cloning:

> There is no "slippery slope" here. The boundary between the two activities is broad and unambiguous. Federal rules and medical guidelines can easily delineate them. . . .

## U.K. Cloning Laws

*In 2001, the British Parliament enacted the Human Reproductive Cloning Act, which punishes anyone who "places in a woman a human embryo which has been created otherwise than by fertilisation" with up to 10 years in prison.*

*Therapeutic cloning does not carry criminal penalties; however, scientists wishing to conduct such experiments must apply for permission to the Human Fertilisation and Embryology Authority (HEFA). On August 11, 2004, HEFA granted such permission for the first time, announcing:*

The Human Fertilisation and Embryology Authority has granted the first licence to create human embryonic stem cells using cell nuclear transfer—a technique also known as therapeutic cloning. The licence will be held by Newcastle Centre for Life. Stem cells created under this licence will be used for research purposes only.

This licence allows scientists to create human embryos by inserting the nuclei from human skin or stem cells into human eggs. In the UK, research on human embryos is only permitted for certain purposes. The purpose of this research is to increase knowledge about the development of embryos and enable this knowledge to be applied in developing treatments for serious disease. This research is preliminary, it is not aimed at specific illnesses, but is the foundation for further development in the treatment of serious disease.

Sources: Human Reproductive Cloning Act, 2001 Chapter 23; Human Fertilisation and Embryology Authority [U.K.], press release, "HFEA Grants the First Therapeutic Cloning Licence for Research" (9 Aug. 2004).

Trying to introduce the cells into a uterus could lead to prosecution. And the regulatory guidelines [could] require responsible government oversight, informed consent by cell donors, a 14-day limit on the growth of early embryos, and a separation of IVF clinics from laboratories for research on nuclear transfer.[142]

## Summary

Proponents of embryonic stem cell research worry that the scandal involving disgraced Korean scientist Hwang Woo Suk will result in a black eye for the contingent of scientists who hope to use SCNT as a technique for creating stem cells. Many see no moral problem with cloning so long as the intention is to create early-stage embryos that are destroyed for research purposes before they are implanted in a woman's uterus. Stem cells from these cloned embryos, it is believed, would have many advantages over cells taken from frozen embryos from IVF clinics.

# The Future of Stem Cell Research

A 10-year-old boy with diabetes had the opportunity to meet with U.S. Senator Susan Collins of Maine. He told her that if he could have one wish granted, it would be to have just one day off from having diabetes. "If only I could take Christmas off or my birthday off,"[143] he said. Like many, he dreams of a day when scientists find cures for diseases previously thought incurable.

Roman Catholic Cardinal William Keeler also has a hope for the future, looking forward to a day when "every human life is respected and defended"[144] and early-stage embryos are no longer destroyed as a source of stem cells.

Are these two hopes incompatible? Opponents of embryonic stem cell research say they support curing diseases, but not at the expense of human life. Some supporters accuse opponents of standing in the way of cures on the basis of religious dogma. Some people, however, are hoping that technology can develop that allows researchers to aggressively pursue cures without destroying embryos. The debate over embryonic stem cell research is a relatively new debate compared with other controversial issues such as abortion or gay rights. It is also poised to change rapidly as new technologies shed light on the effectiveness of embryonic stem cell research and its alternatives. As political developments take shape, the debate over embryonic stem cell research is likely to look quite different just a few years into the future.

## The Impact of Technology

The current debate over stem cell research is deeply affected by the current state of medical and scientific technology. For now, adult stem cells are used to treat various diseases, but more research is needed to determine how flexible they are in terms of creating various types of cells and how long adult stem cell lines can be kept going in the laboratory. For now, embryonic stem cells have not been used to cure any diseases or conditions in humans. For now, scientists have not successfully cloned humans using SCNT. All of this could change in the next few years, however, as technology advances.

For some points of the debate, advances in technology will have no bearing. For example, the moral question of whether it is acceptable to destroy embryos before the fourteenth day of development is unlikely to be answered by further experimentation, writes Harvard professor and author Jerome Groopman. He argues that the question of when life begins is largely a matter of religious belief rather than scientific observation:

> From a scientific point of view, no one can know when ensoulment occurs, or if it occurs. It is a metaphysical question that cannot be empirically answered. In this matter, no data can be sought from experimentation.[145]

In other areas of the debate, however, scientific innovations likely will have a major impact on the debate. What if a respected team of researchers at a major university, for example, announced that it had successfully treated a number of patients with Lou Gehrig's Disease using embryonic stem cells? Pro-life opponents of embryonic stem cell research would likely lose some public support for their position if people suffering from a tragic, progressive, disabling, and ultimately fatal disease were cured with embryonic stem cells. It would certainly be difficult to convince people to pursue alternative treatments such as adult stem cells if a cure were indeed developed. However, that day might never come.

On the other hand, it is difficult to say what type of major breakthrough using adult stem cells would be needed to derail the momentum for embryonic stem cell research. As critics frequently point out, adult stem cells are already in use to treat a number of diseases, but these advances do not get the same publicity as minor advances in embryonic stem cell research, such as positive findings in animal studies. Many critics accuse the press of having a pro-abortion and anti-religious bias. Daniel John Sobieski writes in the *Weekly Standard* that the "liberal press and the liberal media" are "largely ignoring" the greater progress made in adult stem cell research while portraying supporters of adult stem cell research as "heartless Bible-thumpers prolonging human suffering."[146]

The development of SCNT technology will likely force Congress' hand, leading to some form of cloning legislation. To date, Congress has not passed a human cloning ban despite widespread opposition to human reproductive cloning. The sharp division over whether to ban therapeutic cloning appears to have stalled legislation. However, the debate to this point appears largely theoretical. Although for a time it appeared that the era of human cloning had arrived, with the announcement by Korean scientist Hwang Woo Suk of cloned stem cell lines, the revelation of that work as a fraud has returned human cloning to the status of a theoretical issue. Research that was verified, however—especially research in the United States—might give Congress a greater sense of urgency. Certainly a media image of a cloned human baby, were reproductive cloning ever successfully used, would lead to a call for action among an angered or scared public.

# Respect for Life Pluripotent Stem Cell Act of 2005 (Introduced in Senate)

*Responding to the report of the President's Council on Bioethics, U.S. senators proposed legislation to fund the pursuit of technologies to grow embryonic stem cells without destroying embryos. This legislation has not become law. An excerpt:*

(b) With respect to producing stem cell lines for important biomedical research, the Director of NIH shall, through the appropriate national research institutes, provide for the conduct and support of basic and applied research in isolating, deriving and using pluripotent stem cells without creating or harming human embryos. Such research may include—

  (1) research in animals to develop and test techniques for deriving cells from embryos without doing harm to those embryos;

  (2) research to develop and test techniques for producing human pluripotent stem cells without creating or making use of embryos; and

  (3) research to isolate, develop, and test pluripotent stem cells from postnatal tissues, umbilical cord blood, and placenta.

(c) Prohibitions Regarding Harm to Human Embryos—Research under subsection (b) may not include any research that—

  (1) involves the use of human embryos;

  (2) involves the use of stem cells not otherwise eligible for funding by the National Institutes of Health;

  (3) involves the use of any stem cell to create or to attempt to create a human embryo; or

  (4) poses a significant risk of creating a human embryo by any means.

Source: S. 1557, 109th Congress, first session

Another technology that could make a significant impact on the debate over embryonic stem cell research is a method for harvesting embryonic stem cells without harming or destroying an embryo. Such a technology does not yet exist, but the President's Council on Bioethics published a report detailing four proposed technologies. One proposal called for exploring ways to remove stem cells from frozen embryos that were determined to be "dead," i.e., unable to develop into a living baby. Another proposal called for finding a way to remove cells from embryos, while preserving their development into babies. Council member Robert George noted, "If such means can be identified, research involving embryonic or embryonic-type stem cells could go forward, and be funded by the federal government, without ethical qualms and controversy."[147]

Council member Michael Gazzaniga included a terse response to the council's report in which he criticized the proposal, writing that "most are high-risk options that only have an outside chance of success and raise their own complex set of ethical questions."[148] He also expressed concern that pursuing such technologies was a waste of time and money and called for the nation to "move forward with the established laboratory techniques, [which] are already grounded on a clear ethical basis, for studying embryonic stem cell research and biomedical cloning."[149]

Discussing the report, Thomas Murray of the Hastings Center criticized the proposal to harvest stem cells from an embryo that was to be carried to term and born. He writes, "We do not fully understand the risks to the child that might be born if we split some cells off from the early-stage embryo from which the child results," arguing that it is unethical "to subject a healthy embryo destined to become a child to unknown but completely avoidable risks."[150]

## The Impact of Changes on the U.S. Supreme Court

A significant change has occurred in the makeup of the U.S. Supreme Court, which is the ultimate authority on federal laws as well as the interpreter of whether state laws are consistent with the U.S. Constitution. Some day, the court might be called upon to pass judgment on laws involving embryonic stem cell research or cloning. A conservative shift in the court could signal a greater probability of the court approving of restrictions on embryonic stem cell research and cloning.

A change in the political makeup of the court has been coming for quite some time as the nine justices aged. During the 2004 presidential campaign, both incumbent President George W. Bush and Democratic challenger Senator John Kerry made a major issue out of the makeup of the Supreme Court. With several aging justices, the winner of the election stood to have the opportunity to appoint several new justices to lifetime terms on the bench. President Bush promised voters to appoint conservative justices—people who would strictly interpret the Constitution and would be less likely to invalidate state or federal laws. Kerry, on the other hand, promised to appoint justices who would scrutinize laws to ensure that individual freedoms were maintained.

Although judges, including Supreme Court justices, are supposed to be impartial and rule fairly on the facts presented to them, the underlying context in the Bush–Kerry debate was whether, as president, the candidate would appoint justices who would uphold *Roe v. Wade*, the 1973 decision that invalidated state abortion bans. Kerry courted pro-choice voters who wanted abortion to remain largely unregulated, while Bush courted pro-life voters who wanted to see *Roe v. Wade* overturned or at least to see the Supreme Court allow states to have greater leeway to regulate abortion.

President Bush won re-election over Kerry, and in 2005, the prediction about the next president having the opportunity to reshape the Supreme Court proved correct. In 2005, Chief Justice William Rehnquist died, and Justice Sandra Day O'Connor announced her retirement. Rehnquist's death did not have as much significance to the makeup of the court: He had exemplified the conservative judicial philosophy that Bush would seek in a successor. In other words, Bush could be expected to appoint someone with views very similar to Rehnquist's—and he did, with the appointment of Chief Justice John Roberts.

O'Connor, by contrast, was known as the "swing vote" in the Supreme Court. She was involved in many 5–4 decisions, sometimes siding with the court's four conservative justices, other times siding with the court's four more liberal justices. Perhaps the best-known example of O'Conner acting as a swing vote was her vote in *Planned Parenthood v. Casey*, which invalidated laws posing a "substantial burden" on women seeking an abortion. O'Connor had been named to the Supreme Court by anti-abortion President Ronald Regan, and many pro-life advocates expressed disappointment with O'Connor's support of abortion laws. With her retirement, the pro-life movement saw the opportunity for President Bush to appoint a justice who would uphold the states' ability to regulate abortion.

After O'Connor's replacement, Samuel Alito, was confirmed by the Senate, abortion opponents wasted little time in rallying support for state abortion bans. In February 2005, both houses of the South Dakota legislature approved a law outlawing abortion, except in cases in which the procedure was necessary to save a woman's life. Several legislators who supported the bill made comments to the press indicating that the appointment of Roberts and Alito to the Supreme Court gave them hope that the court would overturn *Roe v. Wade* and uphold the law.

If the Supreme Court were to overturn *Roe v. Wade*, the result would not be a nationwide ban on abortion but would instead allow states to ban abortion. Similarly, it is unlikely that any action by the Supreme Court would result in a nationwide ban on embryonic stem cell research. If a state ban on embryonic stem cell research—such as those enacted by South Dakota or Louisiana—were to reach the U.S. Supreme Court, however, it is quite possible that the law would be upheld.

Although abortion and embryonic stem cell research have in common the question of whether an embryo or fetus deserves legal protection, there is an important legal distinction.

*Roe v. Wade* upheld abortion largely on the basis that a woman has a constitutional "right to privacy" that includes making a decision about whether or not to have an abortion. However, as theologian Gilbert Meilaender points out:

> The issue of abortion . . . has turned chiefly on a conflict between the claims of the fetus and the claims of the pregnant woman. It is precisely that conflict, and our seeming inability to serve the woman's claim without turning directly against the life of the fetus, that has been thought to justify abortion. But there is no such direct conflict of lives involved in the instance of embryo research.[151]

In other words, embryonic stem cell research might be on shakier moral and legal ground than abortion is.

On the other hand, writes Janet Dolgin, the images of seriously ill people and their families provides a poignant way for opponents of the pro-life movement to counter the disturbing images of aborted fetuses that the pro-life movement uses to advance their cause. As a result, she writes, "The debate about embryonic stem cell research may be the undoing . . . of the pro-life movement."[152]

## Summary

Nobody can predict for certain where the ongoing debate on embryonic stem cell research is headed. Scientists continue to look for cures using both adult stem cells and embryonic stem cells. If promising techniques are developed using one source or the other, this success will surely shift the debate in that direction. On the other hand, politics continues to play a role in the debate, and with a more conservative Supreme Court in session, the legal standing of embryos might be re-examined, potentially affecting the legality of embryonic stem cell research.

# NOTES ///////

### Point: Supporters Exaggerate the Benefits of Embryonic Stem Cell Research

1  Senate Committee on Science, Commerce & Transportation, "Adult Stem Cell Research," 108th Congress, 2nd Session (14 July 2004) (testimony of Laura Dominguez).

2  Right to Life of Michigan, "The Great Stem Cell Debate: Understanding the Options," fact sheet (undated).

3  See www.stemcellresearch.org.

4  Scott Gottleib, "California's Stem Cell Follies," *Forbes.com* (1 Nov. 2004).

5  Testimony of Kevin Wildes, in National Bioethics Advisory Commission, *Ethical Issues in Human Stem Cell Research, vol. III*. (Rockville, Md.: Author, 2000), p. I-4.

6  Children's Hospital of Pittsburgh, press release, "Breakthrough Study at Children's Hospital of Pittsburgh Finds Adult Stem Cells Show Same Ability to Self-Renew as Embryonic" (23 June 2005).

7  Senate Committee on Science, Commerce & Transportation, "Adult Stem Cell Research" (testimony of Michel Levesque).

8  Ibid.

9  David Prentice, "Adult Stem Cells," App. K to President's Council on Bioethics, *Monitoring Stem Cell Research*. (Washington, D.C.: Author, 2004), p. 331.

10  Senate Committee on Science, Commerce & Transportation, "Adult Stem Cell Research" (testimony of Jean Peduzzi-Nelson).

11  Ibid.

12  Ibid.

13  Ibid.

14  Stephanie Porowski and Emily Elliot, "Adult Stem-Cell Treatments: A Better Way," policy brief (Washington, D.C.: Concerned Women for America, 17 Nov. 2005), p. 9.

15  Ibid.

16  Daniel Callahan, "Promises, Promises: Is Embryonic Stem-Cell Research Sound Public Policy?" *Commonweal* (14 Jan. 2005). Retrieved from Highbeam Research database.

17  Ibid.

18  Tom Bethell, "Mengele Medicine," *The American Spectator* (Nov. 2004). Retrieved from Highbeam Research database.

19  Michael Tanner, "Don't Politicize Stem Cell Research," *Investor's Business Daily* (29 July 2004).

20  Ibid.

21  Ramesh Ponnuru, "A Stem-Cell Defection: A Congressman Educates," *National Review Online* (16 August 2004).

22  Ibid.

23  Charles Krauthammer, "Anything to Get Elected," *townhall.com* (15 Oct. 2004).

24  Leon Kass, "Playing Politics with the Sick," *The Washington Post* (8 Oct. 2004). Retrieved from Highbeam Research database.

25  Tommy Thompson, "Why Bush's Stem-Cell Policy Is Reasoned—And Why It's Working," *USA Today* (15 Aug. 2004).

### Counterpoint: Embryonic Stem Cell Research Holds Great Promise

26  Ruth Faden and John Gearhart, "Facts on Stem Cells," *Washington Post* (23 Aug. 2004), p. A15.

27  Gerald Fischbach and Ruth Fischbach,

"Stem Cells: Science, Policy, and Ethics," *Journal of Clinical Investigation* 114(10), Nov. 2004, p. 1370.

28 Senate Committee on Aging, "Exploring the Promise of Embryonic Stem Cell Research," Senate Hearing 109-191, 109th Congress, 1st Session (8 June 2005), p. 44 (testimony of John Gearhart).

29 National Institutes of Health, *Stem Cells: Scientific Progress and Future Research Directions* (Bethesda, Md.: Author, 2001), p. 38.

30 Senate Committee on Science, Commerce & Transportation, "Adult Stem Cell Research" (testimony of Irv Weissman).

31 Ibid.

32 Gerald Fischbach and Ruth Fischbach, "Stem Cells: Science, Policy, and Ethics," *Journal of Clinical Investigation* 114 (10), Nov. 2004, p. 1365.

33 Ibid.

34 Senate Committee on Science, Commerce & Transportation, "Adult Stem Cell Research" (testimony of Robert Goldstein).

35 Ibid.

36 Senate Committee on Appropriations, "Stem Cells Research, 2005," Senate Hearing 109-249, 109th Congress, 1st Session (19 Oct. 2005), pp. 17-18 (testimony of John Wagner).

37 Senate Committee on Appropriations, "Stem Cells Research, 2005," p. 14 (testimony of Steven Teitelbaum).

38 Senate Committee on Appropriations, "Status of the Implementation of the Federal Stem Cell Research Policy," Senate Hearing 107-874, 107th Congress, 2nd Session (25 Sept. 2002), p. 21 (testimony of Curt Civin).

39 Fischbach and Fischbach, "Stem Cells," p. 1369.

40 Senate Committee on Aging, "Exploring the Promise," p. 16 (statement of Sen. Clinton).

41 Senate Committee on Appropriations, "Status of the Implementation," p. 21 (testimony of Curt Civin).

42 Senate Committee on Aging, "Exploring the Promise," p. 44 (testimony of John Gearhart).

43 Senate Committee on Aging, "Exploring the Promise," p. 28 (testimony of Larry Goldstein).

44 Senate Committee on Aging, "Exploring the Promise," p. 41 (testimony of John Gearhart).

45 Senate Committee on Appropriations, "Stem Cells Research, 2005," p. 18 (testimony of John Wagner).

## Point: Embryonic Stem Cell Research Is Immoral

46 President's Council on Bioethics, *Monitoring Stem Cell Research.* (Washington, D.C.: Author, 2004), p. 76.

47 National Right to Life Committee, letter to U.S. senators (13 June 2005).

48 Testimony of Edmund Pellegrino, in National Bioethics Advisory Commission, *Ethical Issues in Human Stem Cell Research, vol. III*, p. F-3.

49 Ibid.

50 Ibid.

51 Senate Committee on Appropriations, "Stem Cells, 2001," Senate Hearing 107-499, 107th Congress, 1st Session (2001), p. 39 (testimony of Nigel Cameron).

52 President's Council on Bioethics, *Human Cloning and Human Dignity*, p. 156.

53 Ibid.

54 Ibid.

55 Senate Committee on Appropriations, "Stem Cells, 2001," p. 39 (testimony of Richard Doerflinger).

56 Senate Committee on Appropriations, "Stem Cells, 2001," p. 96 (testimony of Nigel Cameron).

57 Senate Committee on Appropriations, "Stem Cells, 2001," p. 38 (testimony of Richard Doerflinger).

58 Ibid.

59 Ibid., p. 39.

60 Ibid., p. 38

61 Testimony of Kevin Wildes, in National Bioethics Advisory Commission, *Ethical Issues in Human Stem Cell Research, vol. III*, p. I-3.

62 Ibid.

63 Testimony of Demetrios Demopulos, in National Bioethics Advisory Commission, *Ethical Issues in Human Stem Cell Research, vol. III*, p. B-3.

64 Ibid.

65 Ibid., p. B-4.

66 Testimony of Gilbert Meilaender Jr., in National Bioethics Advisory Commission, *Ethical Issues in Human Stem Cell Research, vol. III*, p. E-3.

67 Ibid., p. E-1. (Citing Karl Barth, *Church Dogmatics*, III/4 (T. & T. Clark, 1961), p. 424.)

68 Ibid., p. E-4.

69 Ibid., p. E-4.

70 Ibid., pp. E-4–E-5.

71 Senate Committee on Appropriations, "Stem Cells, 2001," p. 39 (testimony of Richard Doerflinger).

72 Senate Committee on Appropriations, "Stem Cells, 2001," p. 47 (testimony of Anton-Lewis Usala).

73 Ibid., p. 38

74 Senate Committee on Appropriations, "Stem Cells, 2001," p. 39 (testimony of Richard Doerflinger).

75 Testimony of Demetrios Demopulos, in National Bioethics Advisory Commission, *Ethical Issues in Human Stem Cell Research, vol. III*, p. B-3.

76 Ibid.

77 Daniel Callahan, "Promises, Promises: Is Embryonic Stem-Cell Research Sound Public Policy?" *Commonweal* (14 Jan. 2005). Retrieved from Highbeam Research database.

**Counterpoint: Embryonic Stem Cell Research Is Compatible with Contemporary Moral Standards**

78 Senate Committee on Appropriations, "Stem Cells, 2001," p. 39 (statement of Sen. Murray).

79 Senate Committee on Appropriations, "Stem Cells, 2001," p. 60 (testimony of James West).

80 Ibid.

81 President's Council on Bioethics, *Monitoring Stem Cell Research*, p. 78.

82 Ibid., p. 81.

83 Ibid., p. 80

84 Senate Committee on Appropriations, "Stem Cells, 2001," p. 61 (testimony of James West).

85 James McCartney, "Embryonic Stem Cell Research and Respect for Human

Life: Philosophical and Legal Reflections," *Albany Law Review* Vol. 65 No. 3 (2002), p. 614. Retrieved from Highbeam Research database.

86 Senate Committee on Appropriations, "Stem Cells, 2001," p. 63 (testimony of James West).

87 Ibid., p. 64

88 Ibid., pp. 64-65.

89 Senate Committee on Appropriations, "Stem Cells, 2001," p. 11 (statement of Sen. Hatch).

90 Senate Committee on Appropriations, "Stem Cells, 2001," p. 60 (testimony of James West).

91 Senate Committee on Appropriations, "Stem Cells, 2001," p. 13 (statement of Sen. Hatch).

92 McCartney, "Embryonic Stem Cell Research and Respect for Human Life," p. 615.

93 Senate Committee on Health, Education, Labor & Pensions, "Examining the Scientific and Ethical Implications of Stem Cell Research and Its Potential to Improve Human Health," Senate Hearing 107-127, 107th Congress, 1st Session (5 Sept. 2001), p. 69 (testimony of James Childress).

94 Testimony of Ronald Cole-Turner, in National Bioethics Advisory Commission, *Ethical Issues in Human Stem Cell Research, vol. III*, p. A-3.

95 Ibid., p. A-4.

96 Testimony of Elliot Dorff, in National Bioethics Advisory Commission, *Ethical Issues in Human Stem Cell Research, vol. III*, p. C-4.

97 Testimony of Moshe Tendler, in National Bioethics Advisory Commission, *Ethical Issues in Human Stem Cell Research, vol. III*, p. H-3.

98 Testimony of Elliot Dorff, in National Bioethics Advisory Commission, *Ethical Issues in Human Stem Cell Research, vol. III*, p C-3.

99 Ibid.

100 Testimony of Moshe Tendler, in National Bioethics Advisory Commission, *Ethical Issues in Human Stem Cell Research, vol. III*, p. H-4.

101 Senate Committee on Appropriations, "Stem Cells, 2001," p. 26 (statement of Sen. Frist).

102 Ibid.

103 Fischbach and Fischbach, "Stem Cells," p. 1370.

104 Senate Committee on Science, Commerce & Transportation, "Adult Stem Cell Research" (testimony of Irv Weissman).

105 Ibid.

106 Ibid.

**Point: Cloning for Any
Purpose Is Immoral**

107 Gina Kolata, "Koreans Report Ease in Cloning for Stem Cells," *The New York Times* (20 May 2005).

108 Press release, Wisconsin Right to Life (June 23, 2005).

109 Press release, Wisconsin Right to Life (Sept. 29, 2005).

110 Press release, Wisconsin Right to Life (June 23, 2005).

111 Ind. Code 16-18-2-56.5 (2005).

112 Wisc. Assembly Bill 499 (2005) (not enacted).

113 President's Council on Bioethics,

*Human Cloning and Human Dignity: An Ethical Inquiry* (Washington, D.C.: Author, 2002), p. 217.

114 Ibid., p. 260.

115 Ibid.

116 United Nations, Hearing "On International Convention Against the Reproductive Cloning Of Human Beings" (Nov. 19, 2001) (testimony of Renato Martino).

117 Senate Committee on Science, Commerce & Transportation, "Cloning: A Risk to Women?," 108th Congress, 1st Session (27 March 2003) (testimony of Andrew Kimbrell).

118 Ibid.

119 Press release, Wisconsin Right to Life (June 23, 2005).

120 President's Council on Bioethics, *Human Cloning and Human Dignity*, pp. 152–153, footnote.

121 Ibid., pp. 162–163.

122 Ibid., pp. 156–57.

123. Ibid., p. 158.

124 Ibid., p. 154.

125 Ibid., pp. 163–164.

126 Ibid., p 165.

127 Charles Krauthammer, "Crossing Lines—A Secular Argument Against Research Cloning," *New Republic* (29 April 2002). Retrieved from Highbeam Research database.

**Counterpoint: Using SCNT to Create Embryos for Stem Cell Research Is Morally Acceptable**

128 Senate Judiciary Committee, "Drawing the Line Between Ethical Regenerative Medicine Research and Immoral Human Reproductive Cloning," 108th Congress, 1st Session (19 March 2003) (testimony of Paul Berg).

129 President's Council on Bioethics, *Human Cloning and Human Dignity*, p. 256.

130 Ibid., p. 130.

131 Ibid., p. 131.

132 Senate Judiciary Committee, "Drawing the Line," (testimony of Thomas Murray).

133 President's Council on Bioethics, *Human Cloning and Human Dignity*, p. 256.

134 Ibid., p. 128.

135 Ibid., p. 135.

136 Ibid., p. 135.

137 Ibid., p. 147.

138 Ibid., p. 149.

139 Senate Committee on Appropriations, "Stem Cells Research, 2005," p. 10 (testimony of Rudolf Jaenisch).

140 Ibid.

141 Senate Judiciary Committee, "Drawing the Line" (19 March 2003) (testimony of Harold Varmus).

142 Ibid.

**Conclusion: The Future of Stem Cell Research**

143 Senate Committee on Aging, "Exploring the Promise," p. 13 (statement of Sen. Collins).

144 U.S. Conference of Catholic Bishops, press release, "Cardinal Cites 'Mixed Outlook' in Fostering Respect for Human Life," (30 Sept. 2005).

145 Jerome Groopman, "Forward,

Medicine! Science, Morality, and Stem Cells" (book review), *New Republic* (1 Nov. 2004). Retrieved from Highbeam Research database.

146 Daniel John Sobieski, "Stem Cell Truths" (letter), *Weekly Standard* (13 June 2005). Retrieved from Hihgbeam Research database.

147 Personal Statement of Robert P. George in President's Council on Bioethics, *Alternative Sources of Human Pluripotent Stem Cells: A White Paper* (Washington, D.C.: Author, 2005), p. 79.

148 Personal Statement of Michael Gazzaniga in *Alternative Source of Human Pluripotent Stem Cells*, p. 76.

149 Ibid.

150 Thomas Murray, "Will New Ways of Creating Stem Cells Dodge the Objections?" *Hastings Center Report* (1 Jan. 2005). Retrieved from Highbeam Research database.

151 Testimony of Gilbert Meilaender, in National Bioethics Advisory Commission, *Ethical Issues in Human Stem Cell Research, vol. III*, p. E-3.

152 Janet Dolgin, "Embryonic Discourse: Abortion, Stem Cells, Cloning," *Issues in Law and Medicine* (22 March 2004). Retrieved from Highbeam Research database.

# RESOURCES /////////

## Books and Reports

Kiessling, Ann A. and Anderson, Scott C. *Human Embryonic Stem Cells: An Introduction to the Science and Therapeutic Potential* (Boston: Jones & Bartlett, 2003).

Maienschein, Jane. *Whose View Of Life? Embryos, Cloning, and Stem Cells* (Cambridge, Mass.: Harvard University Press, 2003).

National Bioethics Advisory Commission, *Ethical Issues in Human Stem Cell Research, vol. III.* (Rockville, Md.: Author, 2000).

Parson, Ann B. *The Proteus Effect: Stem Cells and Their Promise for Medicine* (Washington, D.C.: John Henry Press, 2004).

President's Council on Bioethics, *Alternative Sources of Human Pluripotent Stem Cells: A White Paper* (Washington, D.C.: Author, 2005).

President's Council on Bioethics, *Human Cloning and Human Dignity: An Ethical Inquiry* (Washington, D.C.: Author, 2002).

President's Council on Bioethics, *Monitoring Stem Cell Research.* (Washington, D.C.: Author, 2004).

Snow, Nancy, ed. *Stem Cell Research: New Frontiers in Science and Ethics* (Notre Dame, Ind.: Notre Dame University Press, 2004).

## Web sites

### California Institute for Regenerative Medicine
*www.cirm.ca.gov*
State research agency created with the passage of California's multi-billion dollar embryonic stem cell research initiative. Sets ethical and scientific standards for research and distributes funding for stem cell research in California.

### Center for Bioethics and Human Dignity
*www.cbhd.org*
Conservative Christian bioethics organization opposing embryonic stem cell research and cloning. Offers numerous essays on the topics.

### Christopher Reeve Foundation
*www.christopherreeve.org*
Organization raising money for spinal cord injury research. Favors embryonic stem cell research in an effort to find a cure.

### Coalition for Stem Cell Research and Cures

*www.yeson71.com*
Coalition that formed to support California's multi-billion dollar embryonic stem cell research funding initiative. Offers numerous stories from people suffering from disabling or terminal conditions and explains why they support embryonic stem cell research.

### Concerned Women for America

*www.cwfa.org*
Organization of conservative Christian women, opposing both embryonic stem cell research and cloning. Offers news updates, testimony, and position papers on the topics.

### Do No Harm: The Coalition of Americans for Research Ethics

*www.stemcell.org*
Coalition of scientists and physicians opposing embryonic stem cell research and favoring adult stem cell research. Offers updates on research on the field of adult stem cell research, as well as position papers opposing embryonic stem cell research.

### Family Research Council

*www.family.org*
Conservative pro-family organization opposing embryonic stem cell research and cloning. David Prentice is one of the leading spokespersons for adult stem cells' advantages over embryonic stem cells.

### Geron Corporation

*www.geron.com*
Biotechnology company involved in embryonic stem cell research. Press release archive details the company's discoveries in the field.

### International Society for Stem Cell Research

*www.isscr.org*
International society of scientists involved in stem cell research. Offers basic overviews of stem cell research, bibliographies of scientific research, and summaries of ethical questions.

### Juvenile Diabetes Research Foundation

*www.jdrf.org*
Organization that funds research on type-1 (juvenile) diabetes, including both embryonic and adult stem cell research. Offers information about potential advantages of embryonic stem cell research over adult stem cell research.

### Michael J. Fox Foundation

*www.michaeljfox.org*
Organization devoted to raising money for a cure for Parkinson's disease. Offers information about the potential of embryonic stem cells to provide a cure for Parkinson's disease.

## National Institutes of Health

*www.nih.gov*

Federal government agency that administers a large portion of federal funding for biomedical research, including funding for adult stem cell research and embryonic stem cell research qualifying under the Bush administration's policy. Offers detailed technical information about all types of stem cell research.

## President's Council on Bioethics

*www.bioethics.gov*

Advisory board appointed by the President to study bioethics matters such as embryonic stem cell research and cloning. Offers several in-depth reports on the topics, as well as collected testimony from experts in the field.

## U.S. Conference of Catholic Bishops

*www.usccb.org*

Organization representing Roman Catholic bishops in the United States. Offers significant information about the Church's opposition to embryonic stem cell research and human cloning.

## Wisconsin Stem Cell Research Program

*http://stemcells.wisc.edu*

Offers updates from one of the nation's top stem cell research programs, where James Thompson first isolated embryonic stem cells in 1998.

## Cases and Statutes

*Human Cloning Ban and Stem Cell Research Protection Act of 2005,*
S. 876, 109th Congress, 1st Session
A bill (not yet enacted into law) that would prohibit reproductive cloning but would specifically allow therapeutic cloning.

*Planned Parenthood of Southeastern Pennsylvania v. Casey*, 505 U.S. 833
(1992)
Split decision of the U.S. Supreme Court decision upholding constitutional limitations on the state's ability to regulate abortion. States may not impose an "undue burden" on women seeking abortions.

*Roe v. Wade*, 410 U.S. 113 (1973).
U.S. Supreme Court decision ruling that the U.S. Constitution includes a right to privacy that limits states' ability to outlaw abortion.

*Respect for Life Pluripotent Stem Cell Act*, S. 1557, 109th Congress,
1st Session (2005)
A bill (not yet enacted into law) that would set aside federal funding for researching ways to collect embryonic stem cells without destroying embryos.

*People's Advocate and National Tax Limitation Foundation v.*
*Independent Citizens' Oversight Committee*, Case No. HG05206766,
Alameda County Superior Court (Calif., 2006)
Challenge under state constitution to the funding of embryonic stem cell research in California.

*Stem Cell Research Enhancement Act*, H.R. 810, 109th Congress, 1st
Session (2005)
A bill (not yet enacted into law) approved by the House of Representatives that allows federal funding to be used to research stem cells derived from "surplus" embryos from fertility clinics, with couples' informed consent.

*Stem Cell Therapeutic and Research Act*, Public Law No. 109-129 (2005)
Created a new federal program to collect and store umbilical cord blood; expands the current bone marrow registry program to also include umbilical cord blood.

## Terms and Concepts

blastocyst
cloning
differentiation
egg donation
embryo
fertilization
in vitro fertilization (IVF)
personhood

pluripotent
pre-embryo
pre-implantation embryo
primitive streak
reproductive cloning
somatic cell nuclear transfer (SCNT)
stem cells
therapeutic cloning

## Beginning Legal Research

The goal of POINT/COUNTERPOINT is not only to provide the reader with an introduction to a controversial issue affecting society, but also to encourage the reader to explore the issue more fully. This appendix, then, is meant to serve as a guide to the reader in researching the current state of the law as well as exploring some of the public-policy arguments as to why existing laws should be changed or new laws are needed.

Like many types of research, legal research has become much faster and more accessible with the invention of the Internet. This appendix discusses some of the best starting points, but of course "surfing the Net" will uncover endless additional sources of information—some more reliable than others. Some important sources of law are not yet available on the Internet, but these can generally be found at the larger public and university libraries. Librarians usually are happy to point patrons in the right direction.

The most important source of law in the United States is the Constitution. Originally enacted in 1787, the Constitution outlines the structure of our federal government and sets limits on the types of laws that the federal government and state governments can pass. Through the centuries, a number of amendments have been added to or changed in the Constitution, most notably the first ten amendments, known collectively as the Bill of Rights, which guarantee important civil liberties. Each state also has its own constitution, many of which are similar to the U.S. Constitution. It is important to be familiar with the U.S. Constitution because so many of our laws are affected by its requirements. State constitutions often provide protections of individual rights that are even stronger than those set forth in the U.S. Constitution.

Within the guidelines of the U.S. Constitution, Congress—both the House of Representatives and the Senate—passes bills that are either vetoed or signed into law by the President. After the passage of the law, it becomes part of the United States Code, which is the official compilation of federal laws. The state legislatures use a similar process, in which bills become law when signed by the state's governor. Each state has its own official set of laws, some of which are published by the state and some of which are published by commercial publishers. The U.S. Code and the state codes are an important source of legal research; generally, legislators make efforts to make the language of the law as clear as possible.

However, reading the text of a federal or state law generally provides only part of the picture. In the American system of government, after the legislature passes laws and the executive (U.S. President or state governor) signs them, it is up to the judicial branch of the government, the court system, to interpret the laws and decide whether they violate any provision of the Constitution. At the state level, each state's supreme court has the ultimate authority in determining what a law means and whether or not it violates the state constitution. However, the federal courts—headed by the U.S. Supreme Court—can review state laws and court decisions to determine whether they violate federal laws or the U.S. Constitution. For example, a state court may find that a particular criminal law is valid under the state's constitution, but a federal court may then review the state court's decision and determine that the law is invalid under the U.S. Constitution.

It is important, then, to read court decisions when doing legal research. The Constitution uses language that is intentionally very general—for example, prohibiting "unreasonable searches and seizures" by the police—and court cases often provide more guidance. For example, the U.S. Supreme Court's 2001 decision in *Kyllo* v. *United States* held that scanning the outside of a person's house using a heat sensor to determine whether the person is growing marijuana is unreasonable—*if* it is done without a search warrant secured from a judge. Supreme Court decisions provide the most definitive explanation of the law of the land, and it is therefore important to include these in research. Often, when the Supreme Court has not decided a case on a particular issue, a decision by a federal appeals court or a state supreme court can provide guidance; but just as laws and constitutions can vary from state to state, so can federal courts be split on a particular interpretation of federal law or the U.S. Constitution. For example, federal appeals courts in Louisiana and California may reach opposite conclusions in similar cases.

Lawyers and courts refer to statutes and court decisions through a formal system of citations. Use of these citations reveals which court made the decision (or which legislature passed the statute) and when and enables the reader to locate the statute or court case quickly in a law library. For example, the legendary Supreme Court case *Brown* v. *Board of Education* has the legal citation 347 U.S. 483 (1954). At a law library, this 1954 decision can be found on page 483 of volume 347 of the U.S. Reports, the official collection of the Supreme Court's decisions. Citations can also be helpful in locating court cases on the Internet.

Understanding the current state of the law leads only to a partial understanding of the issues covered by the POINT/COUNTERPOINT series. For a fuller understanding of the issues, it is necessary to look at public-policy arguments that the current state of the law is not adequately addressing the issue.

Many groups lobby for new legislation or changes to existing legislation; the National Rifle Association (NRA), for example, lobbies Congress and the state legislatures constantly to make existing gun control laws less restrictive and not to pass additional laws. The NRA and other groups dedicated to various causes might also intervene in pending court cases: a group such as Planned Parenthood might file a brief *amicus curiae* (as "a friend of the court")—called an "amicus brief"—in a lawsuit that could affect abortion rights. Interest groups also use the media to influence public opinion, issuing press releases and frequently appearing in interviews on news programs and talk shows. The books in POINT/COUNTERPOINT list some of the interest groups that are active in the issue at hand, but in each case there are countless other groups working at the local, state, and national levels. It is important to read everything with a critical eye, for sometimes interest groups present information in a way that can be read only to their advantage. The informed reader must always look for bias.

Finding sources of legal information on the Internet is relatively simple thanks to "portal" sites such as FindLaw (*www.findlaw.com*), which provides access to a variety of constitutions, statutes, court opinions, law review articles, news articles, and other resources—including all Supreme Court decisions issued since 1893. Other useful sources of information include the U.S. Government Printing Office (*www.gpo.gov*), which contains a complete copy of the U.S. Code, and the Library of Congress's THOMAS system (*thomas.loc.gov*), which offers access to bills pending before Congress as well as recently passed laws. Of course, the Internet changes every second of every day, so it is best to do some independent searching. Most cases, studies, and opinions that are cited or referred to in public debate can be found online— and *everything* can be found in one library or another.

The Internet can provide a basic understanding of most important legal issues, but not all sources can be found there. To find some documents it is necessary to visit the law library of a university or a public law library; some cities have public law libraries, and many library systems keep legal documents at the main branch. On the following page are some common citation forms.

## COMMON CITATION FORMS

| Source of Law | Sample Citation | Notes |
|---|---|---|
| **U.S. Supreme Court** | *Employment Division* v. *Smith*, 485 U.S. 660 (1988) | The U.S. Reports is the official record of Supreme Court decisions. There is also an unofficial Supreme Court ("S. Ct.") reporter. |
| **U.S. Court of Appeals** | *United States* v. *Lambert*, 695 F.2d 536 (11th Cir.1983) | Appellate cases appear in the Federal Reporter, designated by "F." The 11th Circuit has jurisdiction in Alabama, Florida, and Georgia. |
| **U.S. District Court** | *Carillon Importers, Ltd.* v. *Frank Pesce Group, Inc.*, 913 F.Supp. 1559 (S.D.Fla.1996) | Federal trial-level decisions are reported in the Federal Supplement ("F. Supp."). Some states have multiple federal districts; this case originated in the Southern District of Florida. |
| **U.S. Code** | Thomas Jefferson Commemoration Commission Act, 36 U.S.C., §149 (2002) | Sometimes the popular names of legislation—names with which the public may be familiar—are included with the U.S. Code citation. |
| **State Supreme Court** | *Sterling* v. *Cupp*, 290 Ore. 611, 614, 625 P.2d 123, 126 (1981) | The Oregon Supreme Court decision is reported in both the state's reporter and the Pacific regional reporter. |
| **State Statute** | Pennsylvania Abortion Control Act of 1982, 18 Pa. Cons. Stat. 3203-3220 (1990) | States use many different citation formats for their statutes. |

abortion, 50–52, 70–72, 122, 123–125
abuse, potential for, 101–103
acute myeloid leukemia (AML), 25
adoption, 48–49, 59, 78–79
adult stem cells
  California and, 37
  David Prentice and, 24–25
  defined, 14
  difficulties with, 40–44
  HSCs as, 22, 40
  Laura Dominguez and, 18–20
  money and, 27
  potential of, 39–43
  rejection and, 21–22
Alito, Samuel, 124
alleles, 108
Alzheimer's disease, 107
amyotrophic lateral sclerosis (ALS), 29, 108, 120

Barth, Karl, 63
benefits, consequences vs., 65–68, 85–87
Berg, Paul, 105–107
Bethell, Tom, 28
birth defects, 34
bone marrow cells, 15, 22, 25
Brinkman, Donielle and Jim, 48–49
Bush, George, 30, 31–32, 44–47, 122

California, 17, 20, 36–37, 114–115
California Institute for Regenerative Medicine, 36–37
Callahan, Daniel, 28, 68
Cameron, Nigel, 53–54
cancers, 15

*Casey, Planned Parenthood v.*, 124
central nervous system, 22–23
Childress, James, 79–80
chimeras, 74, 102–103
Civin, Curt, 43–44, 45
Clinton, Hilary Rodham, 44–45
cloning. *See* somatic cell nuclear transfer (SCNT)
Cole-Turner, Ronald, 80–81
Collins, Susan, 118
commercial motivations, 26–31, 35–39, 98, 114
Concerned Women for America, 25, 27–28
conflicts of interest, 27–28
consent, 114
consequences, benefits vs., 65–68, 85–87
contamination, 44, 45–46

deception, 63–65, 85
Demopulos, Demetrios, 61–62, 67–68
diabetes
  appeals to Congress and, 29
  benefits vs. consequences and, 66–67
  embryonic stem cells and, 38
  insulin production and, 25
  problem of, 69–70
  stem cells and, 34
disease models, 39, 108–109
Do No Harm Coalition, 20, 25
Doerflinger, Richard, 44, 55–56, 58–59, 66
Dolgin, Janet, 125
Dolly, 88–89

Dominguez. Laura, 18–20
dopamine, 23
Dorff, Elliot, 81–82
drug development, 34, 109

embryonic stem cells
  defined, 13–14
  financial considerations and, 26–31, 31–32, 35–39
  Geron Corporation and, 71
  injection of, 38
  juvenile diabetes and, 41–42
  lack of proof of effectiveness, 20–22
  potential of, 15, 34–35
embryos as human beings, 51
exaggeration, 20–22
exploitation of women, 97–98, 114–115

Faden, Ruth, 35
Family Research Council, 24–25
fertility clinics, 13–14
financial considerations, 26–31, 35–39, 98, 114
Fischbach, Gerald and Ruth, 36, 44, 86
Fox, Michael J., 12, 24
Frist, Bill, 54, 85
frozen embryos, 48–49, 56–59
funding, 26–31, 35–39, 44–47, 84
future of stem cell research, 119–125

Galilei, Galileo, 77
Gazzaniga, Michael, 107, 111, 122
Gearhart, John, 35, 37–38, 45–46
gene therapy, 110

genes, 108, 110
Goldstein, Larry, 46
Goldstein, Robert, 41–42
Gottlieb, Scott, 20
Greek Orthodox Church, 61–62, 67–68

harvesting, 122
Hatch, Orrin, 54, 77, 78–79
Hauerwas, Stanley, 64
heart disease, 25, 34, 38–39, 108
hematopoietic stem cells (HSC), 22, 40–41
Holy Trinity Greek Orthodox Church, 61–62, 67–68
human cloning, 89. *See also* somatic cell nuclear transfer (SCNT)
Human Fertilisation and Embryology Authority, 116
Human Genome Project, 28
Human Reproductive Cloning Act, 116
humanity, 52–56, 73
Huntington's disease, 46
hypocrisy, 63–65

identity, twinning and, 73–74
immune-compatible cell creation, 109
immunorejection, 21–22, 109–110
implantation, 72, 77–78
in vitro fertilization, 13–14, 48–49, 56–59, 78–80
Indiana, 94
informed consent, 114
injection, 38–39
insulin, 25, 34, 38, 41–42
intent, 95–98, 107

Jaenisch, Rudolf, 113–114
Jewish Law, 81–84
juvenile diabetes, 38, 41–42, 69–70, 107
Juvenile Diabetes Research Foundation, 29, 41–42, 69–70

Kass, Leon, 31
Keeler, William, 118
Kerry, John, 30–31, 122
Kimbrell, Andrew, 97–98
Korea, 104–105, 120
Krauthammer, Charles, 30–31, 103

legality, 16–17, 57, 91–94
legislation, 84, 91–94, 116, 121
leukemia, 25
Levesque, Michael, 22–23
licensing, 44
life
  beginnings of, 15–16, 49–50, 52–56, 70–78
  definitions of, 113–114
  destruction of, 50–56, 65–68
liver failure, 25
Lou Gerhig's disease, 29, 108, 120
Louisiana, 57

Martino, Renato, 96–97
McCarthy, James, 74, 79
Meilaender Jr., Gilbert, 63–65, 125
Michigan Right to Life, 20
models, 39, 108
money, 26–31, 35–39, 98, 114
monkeys, 106
morality
  abortion and, 125
  advancement of science and, 110–112

benefits vs. consequences and, 65–68, 85–87
destruction of life and, 50–56, 70–77
embryonic stem cell research and, 48–50
intent of cloning and, 95–98
legal protections and, 112–115
religion and, 49, 59–65, 80–84
surplus embryos and, 56–59, 78–80
morning-after pill, 49–50
motivation, 26–31, 43–44
multiple sclerosis, 25
murder, 50–56, 65–68
Murray, Patty, 70–71
Murray, Thomas, 110–111, 122
mutations, 41, 108–109, 110

National Bioethics Advisory Commission (NBAC), 21, 60
National Institute of Health, 58, 79
nervous system, 22–23, 73
neuronal stem cells, 25

O'Connor, Sandra Day, 122–123
oligodendrocyte progenitor cells (OPC), 33
organ farming, 101–102
organic farming, 16
Orthodox Church, 61–62, 67–68

Pandora's box, 101
Parkinson's disease
  adult stem cells and, 23
  genetic mutations and, 108–109

Parkinson's disease
(continued)
Michael J. Fox and,
12, 24
somatic cell nuclear
transfer (SCNT) and,
107
as therapy targets, 15
tumors and, 21
Pedruzzi-Nelson, Jean, 21,
26–27
Pellegrino, Edmund,
52–53
personhood. See life
Planned Parenthood v.
Casey, 124
plasticity, 39–40
pluripotency, 13
Ponnuru, Rammesh, 29
post-natal stem cells. See
adult stem cells
Prentice, David, 24–25
President's Council on
Bioethics
beginnings of life and,
51, 72–73
cloning and, 94–95,
99–101, 107–110,
111–112
embryo identity and, 54
organ farming and,
101–103
research policy and, 31
primitive streak, 73, 75
pro-life advocates, 49–52,
71–72, 113
protection, legal, 112–
115, 124–125
Protestant groups, 62–65,
80
public good, 43–44

Reagan, Ronald, 31
recombinant DNA, 86–87
Reeve, Christopher, 10–12
regulation, 85
Rehnquist, William,
122–123
rejection, 21–22, 109–110

religion, 49, 59–65, 80–
84, 96–97
reproductive cloning,
89–90, 105–110,
115–117
research, 43–47, 56–59
respect, 98–101
Respect for Life Pluripo-
tent Stem Cell Act of
2005, 121
risks
egg donation and,
97–98, 114–115
of rejection, 21–22
transdifferentiation as,
23–24
of tumors, 21–22, 24
Roe v. Wade, 123–125
Roman Catholic Church,
49, 60–61, 80, 96–97

sheep, cloning of, 88–89
slippery slope, 115–117
Snowflakes program,
48–49
somatic cell nuclear
transfer (SCNT)
California and, 36
Dolly and, 88–89
Hwang Woo Suk and,
104–105
legal protections and,
112–113
legality of, 17, 90–91
morality and, 95–98
objections to use of,
91–92
overview of, 14–15
potential for abuse
using, 101–103
process of, 106
reasons for controversy
surrounding, 16
reproductive cloning
and, 115–117
reproductive vs.
therapeutic, 89–90,
104–105
respect and, 98–101

as scientific advance,
110–112
therapeutic process, 96
therapeutic terminol-
ogy and, 89–90,
92–95
Souder, Mark, 29
South Dakota, 16, 124
species, chimeras and,
102–103
spinal cord injuries
Christopher Reeve and,
10–12
embryonic stem cell
research and, 33
injection of embryonic
stem cells and, 38
Laura Dominguez and,
18–20
somatic cell nuclear
transfer (SCNT) and,
107–108
stem cells and, 34
as therapy targets, 15
states, legality in, 16, 17,
57, 90–94
Stem Cell Research
Enhancement Act of
2005, 84
stem cells
defined, 13
legality of research,
16–17
reasons for controversy
surrounding, 15–16
types of, 13–15
uses of, 15
versatility of, 34
suffering, exploitation of,
29–31
Suk, Hwang Woo, 104,
120
Supreme Court, 122–125
surplus embryos, 48–49,
56–59, 78–80

Tanner, Michael, 28–29
technology, 110–112,
119–122

# INDEX

Teitelbaum, Steve, 42–43
Tendler, Moshe Dovid, 82–84
therapeutic cloning, 89–90, 92–95, 96, 105–110
Thompson, Tommy, 32
transdifferentiation, 23–24
tumors, 21–22, 24
twinning, 73–74
type-1 diabetes, 38, 41–42, 69–70, 107

U.K., legislation in, 116
umbilical cord cells, 25
United Church of Christ, 80–81
University of California-Irvine, 33
Usala, Anton-Lewis, 66–67
utilitarianism, 67

Varmus, Harold, 115–117
versatility, 39–40
viability, 76

Wade, Roe v., 123–125
Wagner, John, 42, 47
Weissman, Irv, 86
West, James, 71, 74, 75–78
Wildes, Kevin, 21, 60–61
Wilmut, Ian, 88–89
Wisconsin, 90–91, 92–93
Wisconsin Right to Life, 92–94, 98
women, exploitation of, 97–98, 114–115

Yoder, John Howard, 64

# PICTURE CREDITS

**ALAN MARZILLI, M.A., J.D.,** lives in Washington, D.C., and is a program associate with Advocates for Human Potential, Inc., a research and consulting firm based in Sudbury, MA, and Albany, NY. He primarily works on developing training and educational materials for agencies of the Federal government on topics such as housing, mental health policy, employment, and transportation. He has spoken on mental health issues in thirty states, the District of Columbia, and Puerto Rico; his work has included training mental health administrators, nonprofit management and staff, and people with mental illnesses and their families on a wide variety of topics, including effective advocacy, community-based mental health services, and housing. He has written several handbooks and training curricula that are used nationally—as far away as the territory of Guam. He managed statewide and national mental health advocacy programs and worked for several public interest lobbying organizations while studying law at Georgetown University. He has written more than a dozen books, including numerous titles in the POINT/COUNTERPOINT series.